SpringerBriefs in Philosophy

SpringerBriefs present concise summaries of cutting-edge research and practical applications across a wide spectrum of fields. Featuring compact volumes of 50 to 125 pages, the series covers a range of content from professional to academic. Typical topics might include:

- A timely report of state-of-the art analytical techniques
- A bridge between new research results, as published in journal articles, and a contextual literature review
- A snapshot of a hot or emerging topic
- An in-depth case study or clinical example
- A presentation of core concepts that students must understand in order to make independent contributions

SpringerBriefs in Philosophy cover a broad range of philosophical fields including: Philosophy of Science, Logic, Non-Western Thinking and Western Philosophy. We also consider biographies, full or partial, of key thinkers and pioneers.

SpringerBriefs are characterized by fast, global electronic dissemination, standard publishing contracts, standardized manuscript preparation and formatting guidelines, and expedited production schedules. Both solicited and unsolicited manuscripts are considered for publication in the SpringerBriefs in Philosophy series. Potential authors are warmly invited to complete and submit the Briefs Author Proposal form. All projects will be submitted to editorial review by external advisors.

SpringerBriefs are characterized by expedited production schedules with the aim for publication 8 to 12 weeks after acceptance and fast, global electronic dissemination through our online platform SpringerLink. The standard concise author contracts guarantee that

- an individual ISBN is assigned to each manuscript
- each manuscript is copyrighted in the name of the author
- the author retains the right to post the pre-publication version on his/her website or that of his/her institution.

More information about this series at https://link.springer.com/bookseries/10082

Motsamai Molefe

Human Dignity in African Philosophy

A Very Short Introduction

Springer

Motsamai Molefe
Centre for Leadership Ethics in Africa
University of Fort Hare
Alice, Eastern Cape, South Africa

ISSN 2211-4548 ISSN 2211-4556 (electronic)
SpringerBriefs in Philosophy
ISBN 978-3-030-93216-9 ISBN 978-3-030-93217-6 (eBook)
https://doi.org/10.1007/978-3-030-93217-6

© The Author(s), under exclusive license to Springer Nature Switzerland AG 2022
This work is subject to copyright. All rights are solely and exclusively licensed by the Publisher, whether the whole or part of the material is concerned, specifically the rights of translation, reprinting, reuse of illustrations, recitation, broadcasting, reproduction on microfilms or in any other physical way, and transmission or information storage and retrieval, electronic adaptation, computer software, or by similar or dissimilar methodology now known or hereafter developed.
The use of general descriptive names, registered names, trademarks, service marks, etc. in this publication does not imply, even in the absence of a specific statement, that such names are exempt from the relevant protective laws and regulations and therefore free for general use.
The publisher, the authors and the editors are safe to assume that the advice and information in this book are believed to be true and accurate at the date of publication. Neither the publisher nor the authors or the editors give a warranty, expressed or implied, with respect to the material contained herein or for any errors or omissions that may have been made. The publisher remains neutral with regard to jurisdictional claims in published maps and institutional affiliations.

This Springer imprint is published by the registered company Springer Nature Switzerland AG
The registered company address is: Gewerbestrasse 11, 6330 Cham, Switzerland

This book is a prophetic gift to my son, Bohlale Molefe.

Preface

This book is about human dignity. It imagines itself as an open invitation for a truly global conversation about human dignity among philosophers and ethicists, among others. There is no doubt that the concept of human dignity is as controversial as it is important. Its controversial status, in part, is a function of the fact that the notion of dignity has various or different uses/senses. Dignity can be a feature of being human (human dignity), it can also be a feature of human conduct or comportment (dignified behavior), it can also be associated with dying (death with dignity), it can also be associated with social status (dignitaries), and so on. Its importance can be appreciated at least from two disciplinary perspectives. It can be appreciated *philosophically* insofar as philosophers will try to shed light on what it is that marks out human beings as distinctive, special, and superlatively valuable. It can also be appreciated *politically* insofar as our modern political infrastructure and culture of human rights is built upon human dignity. Our political culture imagines a civilization built on the universal value and status of human dignity.

A call for a truly global conversation about human dignity emerges for several reasons. Firstly, the conversation about human dignity is dominated by ideas from the Western tradition of philosophy. Two such visions of it stand out in the literature from the West. On the one hand, there is the Judeo-Christian vision that accounts for it in terms of the human person being created in the image of god. On the other hand, you have the Kantian vision of dignity that reduces it to our capacity for autonomy. A truly global conversation ought to overcome dependence on Euro-American thought. This dominance of Western perspectives is at the expense of sacrificing and eclipsing us from seeing other visions of human worth. Secondly, this call for a truly global conversation is informed by decolonizing our moral, legal, and political discourses. The aim of decolonization is to bring in more voices and perspectives on this important topic. It is in the context of this cross-cultural engagement that a more global conversation will emerge, possibly with an inclusive and plausible vision of human dignity.

In the spirit of including marginal voices in conversations on human dignity in philosophy, this book draws from salient African resources to think about human dignity. Typically, the ideas of vitality, community and personhood stand out as the basis to think about human dignity in African intellectual cultures. I hope this book will be useful to scholars in Africa and beyond as it explores resources from African intellectual cultures to think about human dignity. I hope it will motivate scholars in and of African descent to join in this conversation drawing from their own cultures. I hope this book can also ignite cross-cultural conversations on the theme of human dignity.

East London, South Africa
Motsamai Molefe

Contents

1 Introduction to Human Dignity in African Philosophy 1
 1.1 Introduction 1
 1.2 The Concept of Human Dignity 5
  1.2.1 The Contested Nature of Human Dignity 5
  1.2.2 The Different Senses of Dignity 6
  1.2.3 The Importance of Human Dignity in Ethics
     and Politics 9
 1.3 Theories of Human Dignity in African Philosophy 10
 1.4 Theories of Human Dignity and Applied Ethics 12
  1.4.1 Euthanasia 12
  1.4.2 Animal Ethics 12
  1.4.3 Disability Ethics 13
 References 13

2 Theories of Dignity in African Philosophy 17
 2.1 Introduction 17
 2.2 Vitality and Human Dignity 20
  2.2.1 African Metaphysics and Vitality 20
  2.2.2 Vitality and Ethical Theory 23
  2.2.3 Vitality and Human Dignity 24
 2.3 Community and Human Dignity 26
  2.3.1 Metz's Principle of Right Action 26
  2.3.2 Metz's Theory of Human Dignity 31
 2.4 Personhood and Human Dignity 32
  2.4.1 The Notions of Personhood in African Philosophy 33
  2.4.2 Personhood as a Moral Theory 35
  2.4.3 Ikuenobe's Theory of Human Dignity 37
  2.4.4 Molefe's Theory of Human Dignity 40
 2.5 Conclusion 43
 References 44

ix

3 African Theories of Human Dignity: Euthanasia, Animal Ethics and Disability 47

- 3.1 Introduction 47
- 3.2 Euthanasia 48
  - 3.2.1 Vitality and Euthanasia 49
  - 3.2.2 Community and Euthanasia 51
  - 3.2.3 Personhood and Euthanasia: Ikuenobe's Account 53
  - 3.2.4 Personhood and Euthanasia: Molefe's Account 54
- 3.3 Animal Ethics 56
  - 3.3.1 Vitality and Animals 56
  - 3.3.2 Community and Animals 57
  - 3.3.3 Personhood and Animals: Ikuenobe's Account 59
  - 3.3.4 Personhood and Animals: Molefe's Account 61
- 3.4 Disability Ethics 62
  - 3.4.1 Vitality and Disability 63
  - 3.4.2 Community and Disability 64
  - 3.4.3 Personhood and Disability: Ikuenobe's Account 67
  - 3.4.4 Personhood and Disability: Molefe's Account 69
- 3.5 Conclusion 70
- References 71

Index 73

Chapter 1
Introduction to Human Dignity in African Philosophy

Abstract This chapter offers a general introduction to the subject of human dignity in the literature in African philosophy. To do so, it does the following. It begins by specifying the two aims of the book. It proceeds to discuss various aspects related to the concept of human dignity in moral philosophy: (1) its contested nature; (2) the different senses associated with it and (3) its importance in moral and political philosophy. Next, it considers the onto-moral resources posited as the basis for human dignity in the literature in African philosophy – vitality, community and personhood. Finally, it highlights the three themes in applied ethics that will be considered in the book.

Keywords Applied ethics · Community · Human dignity · Human rights · Personhood · Vitality

1.1 Introduction

What is dignity, and how might one define it from a truly African perspective? This question forms the core concern and contribution of this book. It explores the concept of human dignity in light of axiological resources in African cultures. The idea of human dignity, roughly, refers to the intrinsic worth of human beings that demands utmost respect (Donnelly 2015). The dominant approach to human dignity, the intrinsic and superlative worth associated with human beings, accounts for it by appeal to the fact of being human, or, at least, by appeal to certain morally relevant ontological endowments of human nature like autonomy (Kant 1996). Since the Universal Declaration of Human Rights, the idea of human dignity has been at the center of our ethical, legal and political cultures (UN 1948; Donnelly 2009; Hughes 2011). One way to interpret the importance of human dignity in our cultures is in terms of it being the foundation of human rights (Freeman 1995). On the foundational interpretation of human dignity, in relation to human rights, the former is distinct from the latter and, importantly, it serves as the ground for it, which means it explains the relevance and role of the latter in protecting and promoting what is most valuable about being human (Habermas 2010).

© The Author(s), under exclusive license to Springer Nature Switzerland AG 2022
M. Molefe, *Human Dignity in African Philosophy*, SpringerBriefs in Philosophy,
https://doi.org/10.1007/978-3-030-93217-6_1

This book has two central aims that pivot on the idea of human dignity. Firstly, it positions itself as *an introduction* to the concept of human dignity in the tradition of African philosophy. The book is *an introduction* because it does not promise to be an extensive philosophical scrutiny of every extant interpretation of human dignity in the literature in African philosophy. It also does not aim to single out one interpretation of human dignity as the most plausible in the tradition of African philosophy. Furthermore, the book does not seek to secure the ambitious conclusion that conception(s) of human dignity in African philosophy are more plausible than those found in other traditions of philosophy. Rather, it is *an introduction* insofar as it seeks to familiarize the global audience of philosophy with the largely under-explored conceptions of human dignity in the tradition of African philosophy. To deliver *an introduction*, the book delimits its scope to the conceptions of human dignity it considers salient in the literature in African philosophy. Specifically, it will offer an explication of human dignity construed in terms of *vitality*, *community* and *personhood*.

The second aim of this book involves the application of these African theories of human dignity to select applied ethics themes. Specifically, and for the sake of focus, I will consider themes in bioethics, animal ethics and disability ethics. The first aim of the book is theoretical insofar as it will be offering a philosophical exposition of salient theories of human dignity in the tradition of African philosophy. The second aim falls within the domain of applied ethics inasmuch as it will be applying these theories of human dignity to select practical moral problems. The book pursues both these aims with the primary goal of providing the reader with a better understanding of African conceptions of human dignity.

A number of considerations inform the two aims mentioned above. The first consideration emerges because the global literature in philosophy is dominated by Western interpretations of human dignity. Take any standard anthology or monograph in philosophy dedicated to human dignity, it will most likely begin by pointing the reader to the Stoic or the Judeo-Christian Christian interpretation of dignity. It will proceed to also draw from the Renaissance interpretation of it, particularly Pico Della's treatment of human dignity, and it will surely pass through the inescapably influential Kantian account of human dignity. It will proceed to appreciate its centrality in the UNDR, and, finally, the reader will be treated to a variety of competing contemporary interpretations (see Malpas and Lickiss 2007; Nussbaum 2008; Rosen 2012; Schroeder and Bani-Sadr 2017). In all these major contributions to the concept of human dignity in the literature in philosophy, the perspective from the global south and, specifically, from Africa, is largely marginal or even ignored.[1]

---

[1] Of all the major anthologies I have read, I am aware of only one that has a chapter focusing on an African conception of human dignity (see Duwell et al. 2014). Of all the dissertations concerned with human dignity that I have come across, none of them consider contributions from African philosophy (see Soroko 2014).

1.1 Introduction 3

The second reason emerges in relation to the growing call to take a de-colonial approach to many of the influential concepts in social sciences, and, if I may add, in philosophy (see Wiredu 1992; Ndlovu-Gatsheni 2020). The call to decolonize surely ought to apply to the concept of human dignity, which has been central to our culture regarding how to conceptualize the special value, or even status, that we tend to ascribe to human beings in our social, legal and political systems (Donnelly 2015; Waldron 2013). An essential component of decolonizing the concept of human dignity necessarily involves imagining and reflecting on it drawing from cultural contexts and resources from marginalized perspectives like that of Africa (Chimakonam 2019). It is for this reason that this book explores conceptions of human dignity drawing from the African context. This project will be invaluable for future research that would be searching for a plausible conception of human dignity, and it is sufficient that I offer an exposition of human dignity in the tradition of African philosophy.

Finally, the idea of human dignity is relevant and useful in a variety of contexts. It is central, as pointed out in the contexts of human rights (Donnelly 2009). It features quite significantly in bioethical debates. In bioethics, it is central in questions relating to stem cell research, abortion, human enhancement, cloning, euthanasia and so on (see Schulman 2008; Sulmasy 2008; Molefe 2020a). It also features in political philosophy and theory, particularly in conceptualizing justice, human rights, capital punishment, egalitarianism and so on (see Rawls 1999; Kittay 2003; Miller 2017; Metz 2012a). It also features in legal or jurisprudential contexts, particularly in matters relating to constitutions of countries, international relations, public policy and so on (see Schroeder 2008). Seeing that the concept of human dignity is interstitial, and is useful in a variety of disciplines and practical contexts, the reader should appreciate the importance of adding an African voice and perspective, which will be a welcome contribution to the literature. It is for this reason that the last chapter of this book will focus on applied ethics, where it will be reflecting on select themes in light of African conceptions of human dignity.

Another reason that informs the emergence, relevance and importance of this book is the fact, as far as I am aware, there is none in the tradition of African philosophy that is solely dedicated to this vital subject.[2] There is no doubt that the idea of human dignity is important in African cultures, and it is taken quite seriously by scholars of African thought[3] (see Wiredu 1996; Gyekye 1997; Ilesanmi 2001;

---

[2]I am aware that Ikuenobe, Molefe and Thaddeus Metz have made important contributions to this subject. Molefe (2020a, b) and Metz (2021) rely largely on the idea of human dignity to reflect on moral and political issues. This book, as an introductory text, brings insights from these scholars and others, to give the reader an overall picture of the status of human dignity in the literature in African philosophy.

[3]If one focuses mainly on the Nguni and Sotho cultures prevalent below the Sahara, one will find that they take the concept of human dignity quite seriously. The amaXhosa people refer to it as *isidima*, the amaZulu people refer to it as *isithunzi*. When a person comports herself well and displays self-respect and generally respects others and social values, she will then be addressed as having *isidima* and/or *isithunzi*. This is one prominent usage of the terms *isidima* or *isithunzi* to pick out human agents with positive behavioral dispositions. There is a sense in which *isidima* or *isithunzi* amounts to a recognition of an inherent divine feature possessed by a human being. This

Ramose 2009; Metz 2012a; Ikuenobe 2016; Molefe 2020a). Some scholars propose religious and others secular interpretations of human dignity (Bujo 2001; Wiredu 1996; Ikuenobe 2016; Molefe 2020a).[4] This book emerges, to respond to the lacuna, by drawing from moral-theoretical resources in African philosophy to explore various interpretations of human dignity and their application to practical problems, thus giving readers an African perspective.

In what follows in this chapter, I provide the reader with a bird's eye view of this book. I structure the rest of the chapter as follows. In the first section, I zoom into the concept of human dignity. In relation to this concept, I will do the following: start by commenting on the contested nature of the concept of human dignity; proceed to distinguish the different senses of the concept of (human) dignity drawing from models proposed by David Sulmasy and Michael Rosen; I will specify the concept of human dignity central in this book; and I will close off the section by discussing the importance of this concept. In the second section, I will give the reader a sense of the three resources in African philosophy to conceptualize human dignity: vitality, community and personhood. In the last section, I zoom into the various concepts that will be relevant in the chapter focusing on applied ethics.

---

divine feature is analogized with a shadow. The idea of *um-thunzi* refers to a shadow, it could be a shadow of a tree, horse and so on. *Isi-thunzi* refers to the special spiritual force that inheres and surrounds a human person. In this light, the notions of *isidima* and/or *isithunzi* are equivalent expressions of the metaphysics and ethics associated with the notion of vitality. The notion of *seriti* found among the baSotho people is equivalent to the notion of *isithunzi*, and it also is associated with the vitality ethics. Though the notion of *seriti* features in many discussions focusing on the moral concept of ubuntu, it is yet to receive the philosophical attention I believe it deserves (Cornell 2012).

[4] Kwasi Wiredu and Kwame Gyekye offer some of the most systematic exposition and defense of moral philosophy in the tradition of African philosophy. It is important to appreciate that these scholars are committed to the meta-ethical view that morality is entirely definable by appeal to some physical aspect of human nature – moral humanism (see Wiredu 1980; Gyekye 2010; Molefe 2021). One would expect that they would logically go on to account for human dignity by appeal to some natural aspect of human nature. In their writings they tend to account for human dignity by appeal to some spiritual property – the fact that we are children of God (see Wiredu 1992, 1996; Gyekye 1992). The story is even more interesting when it comes to Gyekye. In his defense of human rights – moderate communitarianism – Gyekye offers three distinct accounts of human dignity without specifying which is the most plausible. We have dignity because we are (1) children of God or have a divine speck of life, (2) we are created in the image of God and (3) we possess the natural property of autonomy (see Gyekye 1992, 1997). The point remains however, that there are those scholars that account for human dignity by appeal to a divine feature and those that appeal to some natural property. It remains to be seen which interpretation of human dignity, the religious or secular one, is most plausible. This question is beyond the scope of this book.

1.2 The Concept of Human Dignity

The aim of this section is to give the reader an overview of the idea of human dignity in the literature in moral philosophy. To do so, I begin by drawing the attention of the reader to the contested nature of this concept.

1.2.1 The Contested Nature of Human Dignity

A careful reading of the literature on the concept of human dignity will at once reveal its importance and, at the same time, its contested status. The contested status of the idea of human dignity is captured by the fact that it belongs to a group of concepts in social sciences described as *essentially contested* (see Rodriguez 2015). To specify a concept as *essentially contested* amounts to classifying it among those over which there is no agreement concerning its core defining features. The contested nature of the concept of human dignity in the literature in moral philosophy can be conceptualized in at least two distinct ways, one *negative* and another *positive*. I associate the *negative* approach to the contested nature of the concept of human dignity to scholars like Schopenhauer, Macklin, Pinker, Singer, among others.[5] These scholars reject the relevance, validity and usefulness of this concept in moral philosophy. Take, for instance, Peter Singer (2009) who argues that the idea of human dignity is philosophically indefensible and, as such, it should be jettisoned altogether. In addition, consider Macklin's (2003) now-famous view that the concept of human dignity is useless in the bioethical context, and that it should be replaced by the more useful moral concept of autonomy (see also Pinker 2008; Sangiovanni 2017).

The *positive* approach interprets the contested nature of this concept in a way that is philosophically productive, at least in my view. In this view, there is a general agreement on the validity and usefulness of *concept* of human dignity and what it represents. Serious contestations, however, emerge in relation to its substantiation or interpretation. In other words, these scholars draw a distinction between the *concept* of human dignity and the various and competing *conceptions* of it (see Metz 2012a). In terms of the concept of human dignity, scholars agree that this concept captures the deep-seated intuition that there is something morally special about human beings. The contestations emerge, however, when scholars try to give content to

---

[5] In the literature on human dignity, there is an approach to it that is described as a *negative approach* to it (see Kaufmann et al. 2011). I use the phrase negative approach to human dignity differently than it is used particularly in the book by Kaufmann and others. They use this idea to refer to an approach that studies the idea of human dignity in terms of how fundamental harms to human beings *qua* human reveal about it. That is, what do cruel acts like rape, racism, torture and so on, teach us about human dignity. I use this phrase merely to indicate an approach to it that is overly critical to a point of repudiating the term.

what accounts for the moral preciousness of human beings. Scholars account for it differently since they invoke varied onto-moral properties to ground it, such as autonomy (rationality), the image of God, soul, basic capabilities, caring relationships and so on (see Kant 1996; Schulman 2008; Nussbaum 2008, 2011; Miller 2017).

In this book, I adopt the positive view because it is most consistent with the prevailing moral intuition concerning the concept of human dignity in the literature in African philosophy. It is worth noting that I am not aware of the kind of skepticism, represented by what I called the negative approach to the concept of human dignity, in the literature in African philosophy. Scholars of African moral thought, both those that take a secular or religious interpretations of human dignity, express commitment to the idea and ideals associated with it (see Gyekye 1995; Wiredu 1996; Bujo 2001; Deng 2004; Makwinja 2018). I must hasten, however, to point out that this commitment is generally never justified on philosophical grounds. For my part in this book, the prevalence of the moral intuition that expresses commitment to this concept is sufficient to justify the adoption of the positive approach. I will leave it for another occasion to offer a full justification of the commitment to human dignity in the tradition of African philosophy.

1.2.2 The Different Senses of Dignity

In what follows, I discuss the distinct concepts of human dignity in the literature in philosophy. I distinguish the distinct senses of the concept of dignity to avoid conceptual confusion in what will follow in the rest of the book. It is important that I am clear about what I mean when I use the concept of human dignity, and those closely related to it. For example, the reader will note in the book the distinction between *status* and *achievement* dignity. The reader will notice that Polycarp Ikuenobe accounts for human dignity as something we achieve, whereas Molefe conceives it as a value or status we are born with since he defends a capacity-based view. Though both are committed to the concept of human dignity, they are using this term to refer to different things. To distinguish the various senses of the concept of human dignity, I will draw from two conceptual models that I deem to be useful and even plausible. I will draw from David Sulmasy's (2008) and Michael Rosen's (2012) models.[6]

In various essays, Sulmasy (2007, 2008) draws our attention to three distinct senses of the concept of human dignity. He draws our attention to the *intrinsic*, *attributed* and *inflorescent* senses of it. 'Intrinsic dignity' refers to the kind of dignity

---

[6]I select these two models to human dignity because I find them to be very useful for the purpose of this book. For other useful models to distinguish various senses of dignity, consider (Ashcroft 2005; Schroeder 2008; Schroeder and Bani-Sadr 2017). In my view, ultimately these models tend to have an overlapping consensus of how to distinguish various senses of human dignity.

1.2 The Concept of Human Dignity

that tracks merely the status of being human or some distinctive features characteristic of being human. Some scholars refer to it as *inherent* or *status* dignity (Hughes 2011; Michael 2014; Miller 2017). The concepts *intrinsic* and/or *inherent*, in the phrases (intrinsic or inherent dignity), signifies that human beings are born with dignity. In this sense, human dignity is a function of some distinctive endowments associated with our ontological make-up as human beings. Another significant idea associated with the concepts *intrinsic* or *inherent*, in the phrases intrinsic or inherent dignity, is the insight that we do not earn dignity or it does not emerge in relation to any effort on our part, we have it by virtue of being (born) human (Hughes 2011). Moreover, in some sense, intrinsic dignity is inalienable since it is a function of our nature as human beings. In this sense, we cannot forfeit it.

The *attributed* sense of dignity refers to the kind of value that emerges as a consequence human "choice" in relation to attaching a certain status to a set of events or activities (2008: 473). Since the kind of dignity involved here revolves around human choice, we can think of it as "created" since it relies essentially on our recognition for its conferral (ibid.). It is in this sense that Sulmasy accounts for it "as a conventional form of value" (ibid.). We attribute dignity, in his view, to "dignitaries, those we admire, those who carry themselves in a particular way, or those who have certain talents, skills, or powers" (ibid.). In this sense, we can attribute dignity to Lionel Messi, Michael Jackson, Denzel Washington and Obama given the conventional values regulating soccer, music, acting and political leadership, as dignified.

The *inflorescent* sense of dignity involves how the agent uses the distinctive feature definitive of their intrinsic dignity to lead a truly human life. It is a term that captures human or moral excellence insofar as the individual would be living a life expressive of the basic features of human nature and its possibilities. Sulmasy's comment in this regard is quite enlightening when he asserts that inflorescent dignity refers to individuals:

> ... living lives that are consistent with and expressive of the intrinsic dignity of the human. Thus, dignity is sometimes used to refer to a state of virtue—a state of affairs in which a human being habitually acts in ways that expresses the intrinsic value of the human (ibid.).

Human beings that develop the feature definitive of their intrinsic dignity to achieve a state of virtue, which Sulmasy also thinks of in terms of "human excellence", have inflorescent dignity. In this sense, inflorescent dignity essentially involves the nurturing of the capacity distinctive of our human nature. Other scholars refer to inflorescent dignity as *achievement dignity* or dignity as *virtue* (see Michael 2014; Schroeder and Bani-Sadr 2017). It is achieved insofar as we are not born with it. To gain it, we have to enlist efforts to develop habits expressive of the distinctive abilities definitive of our potential for human excellence. We can lose this kind of dignity since we have it only by merit.

I turn now to Rosen's (2012) model of conceptualizing the distinct senses of (human) dignity. In his influential book – *Dignity: Its History and Meaning* – Rosen points us to four distinct strands of the concept of human dignity in the history of Western thought. These include: (1) *high status*, (2) *inherent value* (3) virtue or what he characterizes as "behaviour, character or bearing that is dignified" and (4) "the right to be treated with dignity" (2012: 54 & 58). Dignity as *high status* is associated with Cicero's approach to human dignity that regards all human beings as occupying a special and high status in the natural world, in contrast to animals, since they possess rationality, which secures their "honoured place" in the universe (see Rosen 2012: 12). Dignity as an *inherent value*, usually associated with Kant, involves a certain feature or features that human beings possess that marks them out as morally distinct and special in and of themselves in the universe, hence deserving special moral attention. Dignity, construed as a kind of conduct that is dignified, emerges "as a feature behaviour" (ibid.: 30). Typically, human conduct characterised by virtue counts as dignified. Virtue could be construed in a *weak* and *strong* sense, morally speaking. In a *weak* sense of virtue, it could merely pick out the kind of behaviour manifesting virtues that are properly aligned with the dominant forms of etiquette in that context. Alternatively, in a *strong* moral sense of virtue, it refers to human behaviour expressive of a good character, where the individual exudes (what might be considered as) trans-cultural virtues like courage, kindness, fortitude, patience, friendliness and so on.

Finally, dignity as a right to be treated with dignity corresponds with a *negative approach* to human dignity, where concern revolves around avoiding fundamental harms against human beings *qua* human (Kaufmann et al. 2011).[7] The harms imagined here are those that involve the violation of the essence of being human. Here, I have in mind harms such as *humiliation*, *degradation* and *dehumanization*. The idea of human dignity as a right to be treated with respect or to be treated with dignity focuses essentially on avoiding the kinds of maltreatment of human beings like slavery, racism, colonisation, torture, rape, xenophobia, among others, which tend to instrumentalize, objectify, stigmatize and dehumanize.

Now that I have explained the two conceptual frameworks to understand the various senses of the concept of human dignity, I specify the notion of human dignity that is central in this book and I show how the two frameworks can speak to each other. It is the idea of intrinsic dignity or status dignity that is central in this book insofar as it is foundational in moral and political thought (Sulmasy 2008). The foundational status of this term is justified by the fact that requires us to reckon with the moral speacialness and preciousness of human beings. Typically, scholars account for our value and/or status of human dignity in terms of some ontological property, which they take to be definitive of what makes human beings to be morally special or beings of incalculable moral worth (Donnelly 2015). In other words, our status or intrinsic dignity is a function of our value bearing endowments. In my view,

---

[7] I point out here that talk of a *negative approach* is different from the discussion of it in the section concerning the contested nature of human dignity. Here, talk of a negative approach to human dignity specifies another way to analyse the notion of human dignity, which involves focusing on instances where we suppose it to be most harmed to understand its true nature or character. In this sense, this talk of negative approach is a positive one since it considers the notion of human dignity to be useful in moral and political discourses.

1.2 The Concept of Human Dignity

it is correct to merge the concept of dignity as *high status* and *intrinsic dignity* – remember that Rosen treats these as two distinct strands of conceptualizing human dignity given how they emerge in the history of Western thought. One promising way to merge these two ways of conceptualizing human dignity is to suggest that it is because human beings inherently possess ontological features that make them so morally valuable that they enjoy a high moral status in the universe, above the vegetal and animal kingdoms. In Cicero's view of human dignity that influenced Kant's view of it, it is the intrinsic capacity for reason that secures the high status of human beings (see Waldron 2012; Toscano 2011). I also believe that attributed dignity and dignity as dignified conduct or bearing are equivalent, particularly if we take the weak sense of virtue *qua* etiquette. Inflorescent dignity is equivalent to the stronger sense of virtue, where human beings merit or achieve moral excellence as a consequence of having nurtured the inherent feature or endowment that marks them out as bearers of intrinsic or status dignity. The reader should note that the idea of dignity as a right to be treated with respect will not feature at all in this book.

For now, I have specified that it is the concept of human dignity *qua* intrinsic dignity that will be the primary focus of the book.

1.2.3 The Importance of Human Dignity in Ethics and Politics

To conclude this section, I point the reader to why the concept of human dignity is important in moral philosophy. I make reference to at least three features of human dignity that mark it out as of paramount importance in moral, political and legal discourses. Firstly, the idea of human dignity serves as a moral *constraint* (see Beyleveld and Roger 2001: 29–46). In this sense, to establish that a human being has dignity denotes that certain forms of conduct or treatment towards her are absolutely forbidden without regard to the outcomes or consequences of such actions. The idea of constraints denotes that certain ways of promoting the common good cannot be pursued if they are in violation of human dignity (McNaughton and Rawling 2006). The idea of constraints signals the inviolability of human beings no matter what is at stake, all things being equal (Toscano 2011). In this sense, the idea of human dignity embodies universal negative duties that imposes limits over us in as much as it requires us not to interfere or harm beings of high value in our quest to promote the good. The limitations or prohibitions associated with human beings are quite stringent, if not absolute (Jaworska and Tannenbaum 2018).

The concept of human dignity is important as it also has the *empowerment* dimension (see Beyleveld and Roger 2001). This aspect of empowerment revolves around the duties created by the presence of beings of dignity. Jaworska and Tannenbaum (2018: n.p.) observe that we have *strong duties* to aid beings of dignity. The duties imagined here are empowering insofar as they ensure that beings of dignity have access to resources required to lead decent human lives, at least to an acceptable minimum threshold. For example, the state has a duty to provide minimal structural conditions or opportunities for the development of human capacities like education, public health, opportunities of employment. These are important goods that are necessary for human beings to develop and express their value bearing capacities. The last aspect requires that beings of dignity must be treated fairly or equally. In other words, if we have established that two individuals have dignity then we have a duty to treat them fairly or equally unless there is another consideration that justifies the difference in treatment (see, Griffin 2008; Rosen 2012). Jaworska and Tannenbaum (2018: n.p) comments on this point in this fashion:

> For instance, when distributing goods among such beings [of dignity], in circumstances when they can all benefit similarly, barring special purposes, relationships, or independent claims on the goods, we have strong reason to distribute the goods equally (or in another way that's fair, depending on the account of fairness).

In this section, we explored various aspects related to the concept of human dignity. We considered its contested nature, where we distinguished between the negative and positive approaches to it. I stated my preference for the positive approach, which locates the disputes, not in the concept of human dignity itself, but on the various conceptions (theories) of it. We also noted the various senses of human dignity, and we specified intrinsic or status dignity is the focus of this book, which status one holds merely because she possess the relevant ontological property. We concluded by discussing three aspects, constraints, empowerment and equality, that render the concept of human dignity important in modern moral and political discourses.

In the next section, I give the reader a rough sense of the salient interpretations of human dignity in the tradition of African philosophy.

1.3   Theories of Human Dignity in African Philosophy

In this section, I give the reader a rough sense of the theories of human dignity that will be the focus of this book. These conceptions of human dignity take ground on what in African cultures is taken as definitive of the distinctive ontological capacities of human nature. In my view, which is rooted on a thorough survey of the literature, I identify three properties taken to account for human dignity – (1) *vitality*, (2) *community* and (3) *personhood*.[8] The views I will be elaborating here are associated with

---

[8] It is important at this juncture that I distinguish my approach to the theme of human dignity in African philosophy to that of Thaddeus Metz. Metz tends to focus on community and vitality as the grounds for our human dignity. On my part, I add a third ethical resource as the basis for human dignity in African philosophy, the concept of personhood. Metz offers a naturalist interpretation of the vitality based account of human dignity because he does not find ethical supernaturalism usually associated with it to be suitable for modern and/or multicultural societies (Metz 2010, 2012a). On my part, I insist on a religious interpretation of vitality since I find it to be most consistent with how this idea features in the literature (see Molefe 2018). Remember, in this book, I am not after

1.3 Theories of Human Dignity in African Philosophy

certain scholars in the tradition of African philosophy. The idea of *vitality* refers to a spiritual energy emanating from God, which inheres in human beings; and, in virtue of possessing it, they have human dignity. This view can be associated, though not explicitly associated with human dignity in their writings, with the following scholars Tempels (1959); Setiloane (1976); Shutte (2001); Iroegbu (2005); Imafidon (2013); Molefe (2018), among others.[9] I will draw from these scholars to construct an African religious account of human dignity.

Another way to interpret Afro-communitarian morality or the ethics of ubuntu is in terms of it positing the community, when interpreted in a nuanced fashion, as the final good. A number of scholars of African thought take the interpretation of ubuntu that offers the community as the final good to be plausible (see Paris 1995; Tutu 1999; Metz 2007). There are two possible interpretations of human dignity in terms of the community as the final good. One interpretation of human dignity accounts for it in terms of being a *member* of a community (see Tutu 1999; Metz 2012a, b). Another view of it accounts for it in terms of the *capacity* to form and participate in certain kinds of communal relationships (Metz 2010, 2012a, b). It is the view of human dignity *qua* the capacity for communal relations that will be the focus of this book.[10] Metz espouses and defends the latter view of human dignity as the most plausible interpretation of it in the African tradition. I will draw from Metz's work to elucidate his view of human dignity.[11]

Another resource to account for human dignity in the tradition of African philosophy is the African concept of personhood. The concept of personhood under consideration is the moral notion of it, which identifies "morally sound adults" (Wiredu 2009: 15). The normative idea of personhood refers to a moral agent leading a morally virtuous or excellent life (Menkiti 1984; Gyekye 1992; Behrens 2013). To be called a person, in this sense, is to be morally complimented, admired or praised (Tutu 1999; Molefe 2020b). Two recent attempts at describing the concept of dignity

---

plausibility per se, my aim is to give the reader a picture of human preciousness in light of African thought. Thus, I want to be as close as possible to African cultures in my exposition of these approaches to it to construct their philosophical construct.

[9] I must point out that Godfrey Setiloane (1976) does associate vitality with human dignity.

[10] I do not consider the view of human dignity *qua* mere membership in the community since it strikes me as obviously implausible (see Metz 2012a). In this view, loners and isolated individuals will not have human dignity, a view that is implausible.

[11] The reader might wonder why I do not consider views of human dignity associated with prominent ideas associated with the doctrines of radical and moderate communitarianism, for example. Ifeanyi Menkiti's radical communitarianism does not necessarily or directly rely on a particular conception of human dignity. More accurately, Menkiti does not set out to offer a philosophical exposition associated with the normative idea of personhood. He does mention the concept of human dignity in one of his essays on personhood, but does not dwell on the concept at all. In light of this book, Ikuenobe and Molefe rely on the normative notion of personhood as the basis for human dignity. In this light, one could read these conceptions of personhood as associated with the so-called radical communitarianism. It is also apropos at this stage to clarify that Ikuenobe and Molefe do not agree with the view that describes Menkiti's views on personhood and politics as radical or extreme (see Molefe 2016; Ikuenobe 2017a). When it comes to moderate communitarianism, Gyekye appears to be non-committal over whether human dignity is best construed in terms of spiritual conceptions of it or a secular one.

have appealed to this concept to account for it. On the one hand, you have Polycarp Ikuenobe (2017b) who accounts for it in terms of conduct characterised by the achievement of moral excellence – personhood. On the other hand, we have Molefe's (2020a) view of dignity that accounts for it in terms of the human capacity for virtue. These two contrasting personhood-based conceptions of dignity will also form part of the focus of this book. To elucidate on these two accounts of dignity, I will draw from Ikuenobe's and Molefe's adumbrations.

In the next section, I consider matters relating to applied ethics in relation to the theories of human dignity.

1.4 Theories of Human Dignity and Applied Ethics

In what follows, I consider the applied ethics issues that will be the focus of this book in the African context. I will apply the four theories of human dignity to select questions in bioethics, animal ethics and disability ethics.

1.4.1 Euthanasia

The first applied ethics theme to be considered is in the domain of bioethics. Roughly, bioethics concerns itself with ethical issues occasioned by our biological existence, such as beginning-and-end-of-life issues (see Andoh 2011). On my part, I will limit my focus to the under-explored question of euthanasia in light of these theories of human dignity. Little attention has been devoted to the question of euthanasia in the tradition of African philosophy, particularly in light of the concept of human dignity (see Tangwa 1996; Molefe 2020a). In this book, I will consider the implications of these moral theories for euthanasia. For this book, I will limit my analysis to *voluntary euthanasia*, where the medical patient volunteers or requests for the termination of her own life given her extreme medical condition.

1.4.2 Animal Ethics

One of the central questions in animal ethics is whether moral theories are anthropocentric or non-anthropocentric (Behrens 2011; Horsthemke 2015). Underlying discussions on animal ethics is the growing intuition that animals do or should matter for their own sakes (Horsthemke 2015). Anthropocentric theories of human dignity tend to exclude animals from the moral community. Non-anthropocentric views of human dignity do include animals in the moral community, albeit often only assigning them *partial moral status* (Brennan and Lo 2020). In the book, my aim will be to evaluate the position of each view of human dignity in relation to whether they include (or exclude) animals in the moral community.

1.4.3 Disability Ethics

A major pressing question in moral philosophy relates to the moral standing of people living with disabilities, particularly those individuals that are severely mentally impaired (Kittay 2003, 2011; Nussbaum 2008, 2011). In this book, I will consider whether the theories of human dignity under consideration do include people with serious mental disabilities in the moral community. It is important to recognise that the theme of mentally impaired individuals is among those that are under-explored in African moral philosophy.

Though the book will apply the four African theories of human dignity to these applied issues, I want to emphasize that the aim is not so much to evaluate their plausibility. Rather, the aim is to explore and expose the implications of these African theories of human dignity to practical problems with the hope that it will give the reader a fuller understanding of these under-explored theories of human dignity. I will leave it to the reader to assess which theory or theories they find most plausible or which theories bears the most philosophical promise after sufficient development.

This book has two more chapters, one discusses the four theories of human dignity and another applies them to the cases discussed above. The next chapter offers an exposition of the four theories of human dignity in African philosophy.

References

Andoh C (2011) Bioethics and the challenges to its growth in Africa. Open J Philos 1:67–75

Ashcroft R (2005) Making sense of dignity. J Med Ethics 31:679–682

Behrens K (2010) Exploring African holism with respect to the environment. Environ Values 19(4):465–484

Behrens K (2011) African philosophy, thought and practice and their contribution to environmental ethics. University of Johannesburg. Johannesburg

Behrens K (2013) Two 'normative' conceptions of personhood. Quest Afr J Philos 25(1-2):103–119

Beyleveld D, Roger B (2001) Human dignity in bio-ethics and biolaw. Oxford University Press, Oxford

Bujo B (2001) Foundations of an African ethic: beyond the universal claims of Western morality. The Crossroad Publishing Company, New York

Chimakonam J (2019) Ezumezu: a system of logic for African philosophy and studies. Springer, Cham

Deng F (2004) Human rights in the African context. In: Wiredu K (ed) Companion to African philosophy. Blackwell Publishing, Oxford, pp 499–508

Donnelly J (2009) Human dignity and human rights. Josef Korbel School of International Studies, Denver

Donnelly J (2015) Normative versus taxonomic humanity: varieties of human dignity in the Western tradition. J Hum Rights 14:1–22

Duwell M, Braarvig J, Brownsend R, Mieth D (eds) (2014) The Cambridge handbook for human dignity: interdisciplinary perspectives. Cambridge University Press, Cambridge

Freeman M (1995) The philosophical foundations of human rights. Hum Rights Q 16:491–514

Gyekye K (1992) Person and community in African thought. In: Wiredu K, Gyekye K (eds) Person and community: Ghanaian philosophical studies, 1. Council for Research in Values and Philosophy, Washington, DC, pp 101–122

Gyekye K (1995) An essay on African philosophical thought: the Akan conceptual scheme. Temple University Press, Philadelphia

Gyekye K (1997) Tradition and modernity: philosophical reflections on the African experience. Oxford University Press, New York

Gyekye K (2010) African ethics. In: Zalta EN (ed) The Stanford encyclopedia of philosophy. Retrieved from http://plato.stanford.edu/archives/fall2011/entries/african-ethics

Gyekye K, Wiredu K (1992) Person and community: Ghanaian philosophical studies, I. Council for Research in Values and Philosophy, Washington, DC

Habermas J (2010) The concept of human dignity and the realistic utopia of human rights. Metaphilosophy 4:464–480

Horsthemke K (2015) Animals and African ethics. Palgrave Macmillan, New York

Hughes G (2011) The concept of dignity in the universal declaration of human rights. J Relig Ethics 39:1–24

Ikuenobe P (2016) Good and beautiful: a moral-aesthetic view of personhood in African communal traditions. Essays Philos 17:124–163

Ikuenobe P (2017a) Matolino's misunderstanding of Menkiti's African moral view of the person and community. S Afr J Philos 36:553–567

Ikuenobe P (2017b) The communal basis for moral dignity: an African perspective. Philos Pap 45: 437–469

Ilesanmi O (2001) Human rights discourse in modern Africa: a comparative religious perspective. J Relig Ethics 23:293–320

Imafidon E (2013) On the ontological foundation of a social ethics in African traditions. In: Imafidon E, Bewaji J (eds) Ontologized ethics: new essays in African meta-ethics. Lexington Books, New York, pp 37–54

Iroegbu P (2005) Do all persons have a right to life? In: Iroegbu P, Echekwube A (eds) Kpim of morality ethics: general, special and professional. Heinemann Educational Books, Ibadan, pp 78–83

Jaworska A, Tannenbaum J (2018) The grounds of moral status. In: Zalta E (ed) The Stanford encyclopedia of philosophy. The Metaphysics Research Lab, Center for the Study of Language and In-formation, Stanford University, Stanford. https://plato.stanford.edu/entries/grounds-moral-status/

Kant E (1996) Groundwork of the metaphysics of morals (Gregor M, trans.). Cambridge University Press, Cambridge

Kaufmann P, Kuch H, Neuhauser C, Webster E (2011) Humiliation, degradation and dehumanisation: human dignity violated. Springer, New York

Kittay EF (2003) Disability, equal dignity and care. Concilium: Int J Theol 2:105–115

Kittay EFM (2011) The ethics of care, dependence, and disability. Int J Jurisprud Philos Law 24:49–58

Macklin R (2003) Dignity is a useless concept. BMJ 327:1419–1420

Makwinja M (2018) Human dignity in afro-communitarianism. Dissertation, University of Kwa-Zulu Natal, Pietermaritzburg

Malpas J, Lickiss N (2007) Perspectives on human dignity: a conversation. Springer, Dordrecht

McNaughton D, Rawling P (2006) Deontology. In: Copp D (ed) Oxford handbook of ethical theory. Oxford University Press, Oxford, pp 425–458

Menkiti I (1984) Person and community in African traditional thought. In: Wright RA (ed) African philosophy: an introduction. University Press of America, Lanham, pp 171–181

Metz T (2007) Toward an African moral theory. J Polit Philos 15:321–341

Metz T (2010) Human dignity, capital punishment and an African moral theory: toward a new philosophy of human rights. J Hum Rights 9:81–99

Metz T (2012a) An African theory of moral status: a relational alternative to individualism and holism. Ethical Theory Moral Pract: Int Forum 14:387–402

References

Metz T (2012b) African conceptions of human dignity: vitality and community as the ground of human rights. Hum Rights Rev 13:19–37

Metz T (2021) The need for others in public policy: an African approach. In: Molefe M, Allsobrook C (eds) Towards a political philosophy of needs. Palgrave Macmillan, New York

Michael L (2014) Defining dignity and its place in human rights. New Bioeth 20:12–34

Miller S (2017) Reconsidering dignity relationally. Ethics Soc Welf 11:108–121

Molefe M (2016) Revisiting the debate between Gyekye-Menkiti: who is a radical communitarian. Theoria 63:37–54

Molefe M (2018) African metaphysics and religious ethics. Filosofia Theoretica 7:1–37

Molefe M (2020a) An African ethics of personhood and bioethics: a reflection on abortion and euthanasia. Palgrave Macmillan, New York

Molefe M (2020b) Personhood and a meaningful life in African philosophy. S Afr J Philos 39: 194–207

Molefe M (2021) Partiality and impartiality in African philosophy. Lexington Books, Lanham

Ndlovu-Gatsheni S (2020) Decolonization, development and knowledge in Africa: turning over a new leaf, 1st edn. Routledge, London

Nussbaum M (2008) Human dignity and political entitlements. In: Schulman A (ed) Human dignity and bioethics: essays Commissioned by the President's Council. President's Council on Bioethics, Washington, DC, pp 351–380

Nussbaum M (2011) Creating capabilities: the human development approach. The Belknap Press of Harvard University Press, Cambridge, MA

Paris P (1995) The spirituality of African peoples: the search for a common moral dis-course. Fortress Press, Minneapolis

Pinker S (2008) The stupidity of dignity. The New Republic, May 28. https://newrepublic.com/article/64674/thestupidity-dignity

Ramose M (2009) Towards emancipative politics in Africa. In: Murove F (ed) African ethics: an anthology of comparative and applied ethics. University of Kwa-Zulu Natal Press, Pietermaritzburg, pp 412–426

Rawls J (1999) A theory of justice. Oxford University Press, Oxford

Rodriguez P (2015) Human dignity as an essentially contested concept. Camb Rev Int Aff 28(4):743–756

Rosen M (2012) Dignity: its history and meaning. Harvard University Press, Cambridge, MA

Sangiovanni A (2017) Humanity without dignity: morality, equality, respect and human rights. Harvard University Press, Cambridge

Schroeder D (2008) Dignity: two riddles and four concepts. Camb Quart Healthc Ethics 17:230–238

Schroeder D, Bani-Sadr A (2017) Dignity in the 21st century Middle East and West. SpringerOpen, New York

Schulman A (2008) Bioethics and the question of human dignity. In: The President's Council on bioethics, human dignity and bioethics: essays Commissioned by the President's Council. President's Council on Bioethics, Washington, DC, pp 2–19

Setiloane G (1976) The image of god among the Tswana-Sotho. A. A. Balkema, Rotterdam

Shutte A (2001) Ubuntu: an ethic for a new South Africa. Cluster Publications, Pietermaritzburg

Singer P (2009) Speciesism and moral status. Metaphilosophy 40(3–4):567–581

Soroko L (2014) Uncertain dignity: judging human dignity as a constitutional value. Dissertation, University of Toronto, Toronto

Sulmasy D (2007) Human dignity and human worth. In: Malpas J, Lickiss B (eds) Perspectives on human dignity: a conversation. Springer, Dordrecht, pp 9–19

Sulmasy D (2008) Dignity and bioethics: history, theory, and selected applications. In: The President's Council on bioethics, human dignity and bioethics: essays Commissioned by the President's Council. President's Council on Bioethics, Washington, DC, pp 469–501

Tangwa G (1996) Bioethics: an African perspective. Bioethics 10:183–200

Tempels P (1959) Bantu philosophy (C. King, Trans.). Présence Africaine, Paris

Toscano M (2011) Human dignity as high moral status. Ethics Forum 6:4–25

Tutu D (1999) No future without forgiveness. Random House, New York

UN (1948) Universal declaration of human rights. United Nations. http://www.un.org/en/universal-declaration-human-rights/

Waldron J (2012) Dignity and rank. Archives Européenes de Sociologie 48:201–237

Waldron J (2013) Is dignity the foundation of human rights? New York University Public Law and Legal Theory Working Papers. Paper 374. http://lsr.nellco.org/nyu_plltwp/374

Wiredu K (1980) Philosophy and an African culture. Cambridge University Press, Cambridge

Wiredu K (1992) Moral foundations of an African culture. In: Wiredu K, Gyekye K (eds) Person and community: Ghanaian philosophical studies, 1. The Council for Research in Values and Philosophy, Washington, DC, pp 192–206

Wiredu K (1996) Cultural universals and particulars: an African perspective. Indiana University Press, Indianapolis

Wiredu K (2009) An oral philosophy of personhood: comments on philosophy and orality. Res Afr Lit 40:8–18

Chapter 2
Theories of Dignity in African Philosophy

Abstract This chapter offers a philosophical explication of the theories of human dignity in African philosophy. It begins by pointing out that there are at least three salient grounds for human dignity in the literature in African philosophy – vitality, community and personhood. In light of the onto-moral idea of vitality, human dignity is a function of human beings' possessing higher quantities of it in the natural world. In light of the community interpretation of African ethics, or Ubuntu, it accounts for human dignity in terms of the human capacity for identity and solidarity, or, simply put, our capacity for friendliness. There are two personhood-based interpretations of human dignity. One accounts for it by appeal to the actual achievement of virtue – a performance-based view. Another accounts for it in terms of our capacity for virtue – a capacity-based view.

Keywords Capacities · Human dignity · Friendliness · Personhood · Moral perfectionism · Vitality

2.1 Introduction

This chapter provides a philosophical explication of the theories of human dignity in the tradition of African philosophy. The reader will remember that the concept of human dignity is one that is attended by serious contestations in the literature in philosophy. In my view, these contestations are open to at least two possible interpretations. The one interpretation deems the concept to be lacking in meaning and relevance in moral philosophy. Thus, the idea of human dignity should simply be jettisoned since it is useless, and instead we should invoke more useful moral concepts like autonomy (Ashcroft 2005). Another interpretation construes these contestations involving human dignity as not essentially about the *concept* itself insofar as it captures the moral worth, preciousness or specialness associated with being human. The contestations, on this view, emerge at the point of specifying those aspects of human nature that are believed to constitute or explain the moral specialness or preciousness of being human.

© The Author(s), under exclusive license to Springer Nature Switzerland AG 2022
M. Molefe, *Human Dignity in African Philosophy*, SpringerBriefs in Philosophy,
https://doi.org/10.1007/978-3-030-93217-6_2

On the first approach, it is the very concept of human dignity that is in doubt or dispute. On the second approach, the contestations are on the various conceptions of dignity, as they are an attempt to specify its core defining metaphysical features. The rest of this chapter and book functions in light of taking the second approach to these contestations, which I believe is important inasmuch as it will be adding an African perspective on the discussions and debates on human dignity. I hope it is obvious to the reader that no discussion of *human* dignity can be meaningful without appreciating the centrality of the concept 'human' as its basis. As Jeff Malpas (2007: 19) insightfully remarks – "The question of human dignity is surely inseparable from the question of what it is to be human . . . to attend to human dignity . . . presupposes an understanding of the nature of being human". The contestations pivot on specifying the relevant value-bearing-or-endowing aspects of human nature. Hence, philosophical inquiries and elaborations on human dignity are essentially metaphysical or even meta-ethical in nature. This is the case because they essentially involve the identification of those distinctive ontological aspects of human nature, which mark them out as beings of intrinsic worth or superlative worth (Donnelly 2015).

The concept of human dignity, at least in the dominant view of it, offers a specific way to conceptualize the basis of the intrinsic or high value associated with being human. This value is a function of those metaphysical aspects of human nature that are essential in the project of being human. For example, in Martha Nussbaum's view (theory) of human dignity, human beings are intrinsically valuable insofar as they are endowed with *basic capabilities* i.e., the raw or undeveloped human abilities necessary for human beings to function as the kinds of things that they are in the world (Nussbaum 2008, 2011). Here, by basic abilities, you can think of all the essential human abilities like communication (be it speech or literacy); cognitive abilities (ability to think, solve problems and so on), conative abilities (the whole host of emotions like desire, sympathy, affiliation and so on), among others. In this view, human beings have dignity since they are endowed with basic capabilities.

The global literature in philosophy is familiar with the various metaphysical properties that have been posited as the basis for human dignity in the Western tradition of philosophy (see Waldron 2013: 8). The influential Judeo-Christian view tends to specify some spiritual properties as the basis for human dignity, be it the soul or the image of God (see Schulman 2008). The most influential secular view of human dignity in the West, usually associated with Immanuel Kant, which historically can be traced from the Stoics (like Seneca), to the Renaissance thinkers (like Pico Della), accounts for it by appeal to the human ability for rationality or autonomy (see Rosen 2012; Schroeder and Bani Sadr 2017). One can also appreciate emerging views of human dignity as espoused, for example, by feminists, which tend to account for it by appeal to certain kinds of interpersonal relationships, or at least abilities to participate and/or benefit from such social relationships, specifically those characterized by dependency as their defining moral feature (see Kittay 2005; Miller 2017).

This book emerges largely because the literature in moral philosophy is generally not familiar with African visions of human nature and their implications for human dignity. In this chapter, I specify three salient grounds for human dignity in the tradition of African philosophy. I will draw a distinction between religious and

2.1 Introduction   19

secular approaches to human dignity. In this chapter, I will consider one religious interpretation of human dignity and two secular theories of it. By 'religious', in this instance, I am referring to those views of morality that ground it on a spiritual property. A property is 'spiritual' insofar as it is divine or is intrinsically connected with a supra-sensible being like God. The common religious rendition of human dignity in some African traditions ground it on the metaphysical property of vitality or life force, or simply life.

Another salient view of human dignity in the tradition of African philosophy grounds it on the distinctive human ability to participate in harmonious relationships – the relational or community view of human dignity. The final view of human dignity grounds it on the normative concept of personhood. There are two competing interpretations of the personhood-based view of human dignity in the literature. The one view of personhood accounts for human dignity in terms of the *actual* achievement or expression of moral excellence. The other view explains human dignity by appeal to the human *capacity* that informs the very possibility of acquiring moral excellence, rather than on the actual achievement of human excellence.

Several clarifications are urgent and necessary before I delve into the details of each of the respective African theories of human dignity. Firstly, I stated above that adumbrations on human dignity essentially involve some view of human nature since it (*human* dignity) is a function of those distinctive ontological aspects of human nature. That said, I need to clarify that it is not the aim of this chapter to give an exhaustive analysis of the African views of human nature (see Kaphagawani 2004). Neither do I aim to defend any such views of human nature. My task is a simple one. I will solely focus on the relevant metaphysical property usually posited as the basis for human dignity without getting into the whole story regarding conceptions of human nature associated with it. Secondly, I remind the reader that this project is largely expository rather than argumentative in nature. I will not, in this project, claim or even attempt to justify the view that any of the theories of human dignity to be considered here is more plausible than others. There is no implicit suggestion also that these views are better than those in any other tradition of philosophy. The goal of this chapter and book involves merely familiarizing readers with the under-explored philosophical accounts of human dignity in the tradition of African philosophy. The aim is to explain them in as simple or as accessible a fashion as possible.

I divide this chapter into three major sections. Each section is dedicated to each of the grounds posited, in the literature in African philosophy, as the basis for human dignity – vitality, harmony and personhood. In total, I will consider four theories of human dignity. I will do so because there are two competing interpretations of human dignity associated with the personhood-based account of it in the literature. The first section will unfold the vitality based view of human dignity. The second section will focus on the relational (community) view of human dignity. The third section will expound the personhood based accounts of human dignity – the performance-and capacity based views of it. Furthermore, to ensure that our philo-sophical exposition of the theories of human dignity is meaningful, I will contextu-alize the discussion of each theory by providing the reader with the relevant theoretical details, be it metaphysical or moral, as I deem fit and necessary to offer lucid accounts of dignity. In relation to a vitality-based account of human dignity, I will furnish the reader with a sketch of the overall metaphysical system that houses this concept and the ethical theory usually associated with it. On the relational view of human dignity, I will begin by offering an explication of how this account appeals to the notion of community or harmony (which terms are used interchangeably) to account for a principle of right action. In relation to the personhood-based accounts, I will begin by providing a general account of personhood as a basis for moral theory.

In what follows, I consider the onto-moral notion of vitality and its conception of human dignity.

2.2 Vitality and Human Dignity

In this section, I consider a religious interpretation of human dignity. In a sense, I am venturing into African religious ethics, specifically with the aim to articulate an African religious theory of human dignity. To do so, I will rely on the dominant onto-moral category of vitality. 'Vitality' refers to a spiritual energy that originates and maximally inheres in God, who has since distributed it to all that exists in the world. To properly appreciate the vitality-based view of human dignity, I suggest that we need to do two tasks. Firstly, I will give the reader some understanding of the overall metaphysical scheme within which the concept of vitality inheres and operates. This task is important given the assumption that religious ethics "*is incomplete without metaphysics*, that is, critical reflection on the character of reality. . . " (Gamwell 2005: 112, emphasis). Unfolding the metaphysics of vitality will help the reader to appreciate the order and structure of reality that informs its normative orientation. Secondly, I will provide a sketch of ethical theory associated with vitality. Let's turn to African metaphysics as it relates to vitality.

2.2.1 African Metaphysics and Vitality

A common way to conceptualize reality in African metaphysical thought is characterized by three features, namely: metaphysical monism, metaphysical holism and vitalism (see Molefe 2015a, b). In my understanding of African metaphysics, metaphysical monism emerges both as a negative and positive thesis. As a negative thesis, it emerges in the context of decolonizing African thought, particularly from the influential European metaphysics that tends to be characterized by a variety of dualisms. One common example of this dualism is the distinction between the mind and body that has characterized philosophical disquisitions of human nature and of the mind (see Wiredu 1996), another is the bifurcation of being into substance and accidents (see Asouzu 2007; Chimakonam and Ogbonnaya 2021). The complaint here, by African philosophers, is that a careful analysis of African metaphysics will reveal that there are no such strict dichotomies such as body and mind, substance and

2.2 Vitality and Human Dignity

accidents, heaven and hell, flesh and spirit and so on (Shutte 1993). Positively, metaphysical monism, is claim that there is a single realm of reality, the cosmos, within which everything exists and holds together.

A commitment to metaphysical monism is not tantamount to denying the distinction between the natural and supernatural stuff in the world. Rather, it is to appreciate that both the natural and supernatural stuff are a part of a single cosmos or whole. By 'natural' properties I am referring to those aspects of reality that we can access by appeal to scientific recourse, whereas 'supernatural' ones are those that lie beyond the reach of scientific means. In African metaphysical thought, the world as we know it is constituted by both physical and spiritual things. All the things that constitute the furniture of the world are contained within the same cosmos. God, ancestors, spirits along with all the natural things like us human beings, animals, trees, mountains are continuous and contiguous as part of the same world.

The idea of *metaphysical holism* is a view regarding how to perceive the relationships, if at all, between things in the world. The reader might here recall the distinction between analytic and holistic approaches (Nisbett et al. 2001). Analytic approaches tend to perceive things individually and independently of each other. Think of the dominant scientific approach that tends to analyze things to their most basic component to make sense of them. One can take any object and analytically break it down until they arrive at an atom, which is its basic constituent component. Holistic approaches, on the other hand, tend to perceive things in terms of how they hang and function together in relationships. Holistic approaches tend to take a relational approach to perceive and interpret reality, where the concepts of interrelation and interdependence play a centrally defining role. Notice this comment by Verhoef and Michel (1997: 395) on metaphysical holism in light of African thought – "Everything – God, ancestors, humans, animals, plants and inanimate objects – is connected, interdependent and interrelated". For another illuminating comment on metaphysical holism consider Felix Munyadzaradzi Murove (2009: 29):

> African ethics arises from an understanding of the world as an interconnected whole . . . This relatedness blurs the distinction between humanity and nature, the living and the dead, the divine and the human.

Nel (2008: 37–38) further informs us that African metaphysics is characterized by "the integration of three distinguishable aspects, namely, the environment, society, and the spiritual".

In light of the above, we see here an interesting metaphysical picture. We have a single continuum of reality – the cosmos. This reality is composed of distinct kinds of objects. Following Nel, we can divide this reality into three kinds of things – the environment, social and spiritual communities. Though we can conceptually distinguish these three elements constituting an African metaphysical scheme, we should always understand them ultimately in terms of their interdependence. To exist just is to be caught up in a flux of interdependent relationships. The relationship of interdependence between these different spheres of existence is typically represented in a spherical or hierarchical fashion (see Menkiti 1984, 2004; Shutte 2001). The common representation in the literature, however, is a hierarchical one. Laurenti Magesa (1997: 39) affirms the hierarchical rendition in this fashion:

> In the conception of African religion, the universe is a composite of divine, spirit, human, animate and inanimate elements, hierarchically perceived, but directly related, and always interacting with one another.

Firstly, notice, Magesa affirms the holistic conceptions of reality in African thought by construing the universe as a *composite*. The notion of a 'composite' denotes things that are fused or amalgamated, which precisely captures the logic of holistic approaches. Notice, he goes on to accentuate that these elements are related and are always interacting, to suggest that they cohere in some kind of interrelating set of relationships. Secondly, he understands the elements (divine, spirit, human, animate and inanimate) that composes reality to stand in some kind of hierarchy. Two crucial questions can be raised in this context. The first question pertains to what explains the interconnectedness of things in the universe. The second one revolves around what informs the position of each entity in the hierarchy.

The standard answer to both of these questions resides in the concept of vitality. Remember that vitality is a spiritual energy that originates from God, and God has since distributed it to all existing things albeit in varying quantities (Dzobo 1992a, b; Attoe 2020). With regards to the first question, the notion of vitality serves as the glue that connects things together. In other words, things can interact or affect each other (in whatever way) because they possess vitality. It is the fact that everything has vitality that explains why they can interact in the first place. One useful analogy to explain the interactive aspect of vitality is to conceive of each existing thing as magnetic field always open and ready to connect with others (see Shutte 1993; Imafidon 2013).

The answer to the second question concerning how to determine the status of each object in the hierarchy is a function of the quantity of vitality it possesses (see Imafidon 2013: 40). More accurately. the dominant view is that the very order and structure of the hierarchy is a function of God's distribution of vitality. Divine order and will, on this view, revolves around the hierarchy and the position each entity occupies in it. God holds the highest position in the hierarchy because vitality originates and maximally inheres in him. After God, follows ancestors, another member of the spiritual community, which possesses higher quantities of vitality. At the heart or centre of the hierarchy is human beings. Human beings possess lower quantities than members of the spiritual community. It is crucial, however, to notice that human beings possess the highest quantity of vitality in the natural sphere. After human beings, what follows is the animate kingdom, which possesses lower forms of vitality. Here you can think of animals, birds and so on. Inanimate objects possess the lowest quantity of vitality (see Magesa 1997; Wiredu 1996; Shutte 2001; Molefe 2018).

Now that we have a rough picture of the ontological scheme that grounds the notion of vitality, we can proceed to roughly consider an ethical theory associated with it. By ethical theory, in this instance, I have three distinct things in mind. Firstly, I have a (meta-ethical) account of the nature of moral properties. Secondly, I have a normative theory. Finally, I have a theory of human dignity. I go into all this trouble of being a bit detailed for the sake of a global readership that may not be familiar with both the metaphysics and ethics associated with vitality.

2.2.2 *Vitality and Ethical Theory*

One meta-ethical question that might take our attention involves the nature of moral properties, whether they are natural (ethical-naturalism) or supernatural (ethical-supernaturalism). If we take vitality as the ground for morality then it follows that moral properties are essentially spiritual. This is the case because the property of vitality is one that emanates from God and is therefore divine by nature. Now that we know that the moral properties are spiritual, we still need an account that specifies what constitutes rightness or wrongness in terms of vitality. For example, the influential Divine Command Theory (DCT) accounts for morality in terms of God's will (Rachels and Rachels 2015). Specifically, God's will is defined by what he commands or forbids. In this context, rightness is a function of what God commands and wrongness is a function of what He forbids (Idziak 1980).

In light of vitality, morality *qua* specifying what constitutes rightness and wrongness is a function of a positive and negative relation to vitality, respectively. A relation is *positive* in relation to vitality (hence, constituting rightness) insofar as it increases or nurtures vitality, or more life. A relation is *negative* in relation to vitality (hence constituting wrongness) insofar as it leads to the deterioration or diminishing of vitality, or leads to death. This comment by Placide Tempels (1959: 158, emphasis mine) affirms this interpretation:

> The key principle of Bantu philosophy is that of vital force. *The activating and final aim of all Bantu effort is only the intensification of vital force.* To protect it or to increase vital force, that is the motive or profound meaning in all their practices. It is the ideal which animates the life of the '*muntu*', the only thing for which he is ready to suffer and to sacrifice himself

On this view, morality is understood strictly in terms of some kind of relation to vitality, whether the agent intensifies or diminishes it. In light of vitality ethics, morality is essentially about the triumph of life (which is achieved by the intensification of vitality) over death (Magesa 1997). To better appreciate the definition of morality (in terms of the intensification of life force) it is crucial that we clarify the notion of death in this context. This is the case because morality is construed in a context where there is an "antithesis between life and death", in which life (vitality and its intensification) is "permanently threatened by death" (Bujo 2009: 281–282). On this view, death represents the worst moral evil (Bujo 2005). The notion of death is generally understood in two forms on this view. The one form of it is *processual* and the other *absolute* (Bikopo and van Bogaert 2009). *Processual death* involves the state where one's vitality is decreasing or diminishing largely due to their agency. *Absolute death* refers to a state where one has completely shed her vitality i.e., has reached a status where they completely lost their vitality. In this light, the essence of morality is acquiring and/or preserving vitality and an immoral one is a function of depleting one's vitality.

Now that we have a meta-ethical picture associated with vitality, we can proceed to consider normative theories associated with it. I identify at least three possible normative theories in relation to vitality, namely: a consequentialist, deontological and a perfectionist interpretation renditions of vitality (see Metz 2012b, 2021;

Molefe 2018). Roughly, a *consequentialist* principle of right action accounts for it in terms of actions that maximize vitality i.e., make sure that there is as much vitality as is possible. A deontological principle accounts for it in terms of actions that honour vitality. A *perfectionist* interpretation accounts for permissible actions in terms of those actions that perfect one's character, by way of acquiring more vitality.

2.2.3 Vitality and Human Dignity

I am the first to admit that the above exposition of African metaphysics and ethical theory associated with vitality is sketchy and rough. I also believe that it suffices for our purpose of articulating a vitality based account of human dignity. Below, I draw the attention of the reader to quotations that explain how things come to possess internal or intrinsic value in the ethical discourse of vitality. Notice Pantaleon Iroegbu's (2005: 448) comment:

> This brings to focus the positive value of life. Because it is divine in resemblance, it must be taken loftly and with highest respect. It must be seen for what it is: of high value.

For another, consider this remark:

> In the case of Bantu philosophy, the ontological base is the concept of energy, strength, and vital force. *It is what gives beings their intrinsic value* (Bikopo and van Bogaert 2009: 44, emphasis mine).

These quotations affirm the centrality of vitality in African ethical thought. Above, we also noted that the possession of vitality is positive, invites respect for those things that possess it. Moreover, we notice that we here have an account of how things come to have intrinsic value. We are informed that the mere possession of vitality is sufficient for any entity to be valuable in itself. In other words, any and all objects that possess vitality, no matter the quantity, are intrinsically valuable. It is crucial, however, to appreciate that to assert that everything is intrinsically valuable since all that exists possess vitality is not tantamount to the view that everything in the cosmos has dignity.

On the vitality ethical theory, although everything has intrinsic value, it is only human beings that have dignity. I provide two reasons to clarify and justify this claim. Firstly, I urge the reader to remember the technical distinction between moral status and dignity. The notion of moral status comes in degrees, at least in the common formulation of it and the one I favour (see DeGrazia 2008; Toscano 2011). The highest form of moral status is tantamount to dignity. Those entities with lesser forms of vitality merely have moral status and those with higher (like human beings in the natural domain) have dignity. In light of the metaphysical hierarchy associated with vitality, we assign human beings with full moral status (dignity) and we accord the animate and inanimate forms of life with partial and lower moral status, respectively. The reason for this is that we are aware that on this moral scheme "the theatre of morality and ethical responsibility is the visible world" (Magesa 1997: 72).[1] If the domain of the moral is delimited to the visible part of the cosmos, we know that human beings possess the highest forms of vitality in the visible sphere of the cosmos. Metz (2012b: 24) affirms this view – "Within this metaphysical picture, which is common below the Sahara, human dignity can be understood to be constituted by the fact that, of physical beings, we have the most life-force."

This view of human dignity emerges in light of appreciating that within the cosmos, there is a physical (visible) and spiritual (invisible) realm. We are informed that morality occurs in the context of the visible realm, and we also know that human beings possess the highest quantities of vitality in this realm, hence we assign them human dignity. Another way this idea of the physical realm being the theatre of morality is captured in this fashion – "Since the universal order exists for the sake of human life, humanity is *its most important element* or aspects, its centre" (ibid, see Mbiti 1969a: 33, emphasis mine). We are informed that humanity is the most important element of the universe. The idea that human beings are the most important beings in the visible universe leads us to the second reason that explains why human beings have dignity.

The second reason, in line with the above quotations, captures the view that in the common formulation of African metaphysical thought, human beings occupy a special place that a mountain, forest, bird, ancestors or even God cannot occupy. Elvis Imafidon (2013: 42) makes this comment in relation to the position of human beings in the hierarchy:–

> The person occupies a central place in an African thought system because (other) entities find meaning in his/her life.

Benezet Bujo (2005: 454) expresses a similar thought when he observes:

> All the elements in the universe imply each other and interlock. One cannot touch one of them without causing the whole to vibrate. Humans are not only part of the cosmos, but they are also the *summary* of its totality, so to speak.

In another place, citing Mveng, Bujo (2009: 282) observes that:

> Within this hierarchy of forces, the human person appears as, the synthesis of the whole universe, (she) is considered a microcosm within a macrocosm. The African there conceives of personal salvation as being connected to the cosmos . . .

Unlike all other elements in the universe only human beings serve as the summary of its totality. The idea of human beings serving as the summary of the cosmos, in my view, expresses the moral specialness of human beings (their dignity) in the universe. In the Christian tradition, the human worth or moral specialness of human beings *qua* the status of dignity is a function of them being created in the image of God. In the African tradition, if I were to use the language analogous to the Christian

---

[1] The idea here seems to be that God and ancestors are morally perfect. Morality, properly speaking, is the responsibility and a challenge that revolves around human beings. And, in an important sense, the moral condition of the world, understood broadly to include all natural things, depends on human beings as moral agents. In this light, the physical sphere is the theatre of morality.

tradition, human beings are the image or representative of all spheres of reality – the divine, the social and environmental. It is precisely because human beings are the image of the cosmos that their "actions in relation to (the) community and nature are central to the ability to create harmony" (Imafidon 2013: 44). Moreover, Godfrey Onah (2013: n.p) informs us that "Living harmoniously within a community is therefore a moral obligation ordained by God for the promotion of life." The ethical insight here is that unlike any other entity in the physical sphere, only human beings have the capacity and duty to ensure equilibrium and harmony among all the three spheres of existence, obviously with the help from the spiritual community. Remember, harmonious interaction is essential for intensifying vitality.

Above, I discussed the metaphysics and ethics associated with vitality. I went on to specify an account of human dignity associated with vitality, which revolves around them occupying the highest sphere in the physical realm and also being the image of the cosmos insofar as they alone can most effect the divine and moral goal of maintaining harmony in the universe.[2] I turn now to consider the community-based view of human dignity.

2.3 Community and Human Dignity

There is no doubt that Thaddeus Metz has made a significant contribution to ethical theory in the tradition of African philosophy. In what follows, I will focus mainly on two aspects of his theorization in value theory in the tradition of African philosophy. I will first give the reader a rough sense of his theory of right action. I begin with his theory of right action to give the reader a sense of how Metz construes African ethics. It is interesting to note that Metz's moral philosophy, when evaluating his overall contribution to African ethics, began by constructing what he considers to be, at least, a promising African normative theory (see Metz 2007a, b). Of late, he has come to believe this account to be plausible and to warrant serious consideration in the literature, albeit after ameliorating it significantly (see Jones and Metz 2015; Metz 2021). With a normative theory, as a foundational basis for his moral philosophy, I will proceed to articulate his theory of moral status and/or human dignity.

2.3.1 Metz's Principle of Right Action

As a point of departure, I inform the reader that Metz is committed to "ethical naturalism" as definitive of African ethics – a secular approach to morality (Metz 2007a: 328). If morality is characteristically definable by some natural property then

---

[2] In the rest of the chapter and book, I will rely on the first interpretation of human dignity, which accounts for it in terms of human beings possessing higher quantities of it.

2.3 Community and Human Dignity

it behooves us to consider which one does the job of accounting for morality in his ethical theory. To get an answer to this question, Metz appeals to the ethical concept of Ubuntu salient among the Bantu speaking people in many parts of Africa below the Sahara (Eze 2005; LenkaBula 2008). The concept of Ubuntu is generally associated with the maxim 'a person is a person through other persons'. There are many ethical insights that can be drawn from this maxim.

One aspect of it that Metz believes should catch our attention is that it defines morality by appeal to certain interpersonal relationships. Morality, in this view, is a communal or relational enterprise, which means it is impossible outside of social relationships. In one place, Metz draws a sharp distinction between moral theories that ground morality in a feature intrinsic to an individual and those that locate it external to her. In keeping with the communitarian orientation of African cultures, Metz favors an account of morality that locates the good in a property external to the individual. In his search for a plausible African normative theory, Metz identifies six basic norms. In the context of this search, he makes the following profound observation:

> Before turning to the remaining two accounts of ubuntu as a moral theory, notice that the above four ground morality in *something internal to the individual*, whether it be her life (U1), well-being (U2), rights (U3), or self-realization (U4). A different understanding of the morality of ubuntu includes the idea *that moral value fundamentally lies not in the individual, but rather in a relationship between individuals* (2007a: 331, emphasis mine).

Interestingly, Metz observes that many interpretations of African ethics tend to account for it by appeal to some internal property of the individual like life, well-being, self-realization and so on. In Metz's view of African ethics, a plausible interpretation of morality, given its communitarian orientation, ought to account for it by appeal to a property external to the individual, specifically a relationship between individuals. The important task now is to unfold the precise nature of the kinds of social relationships definitive of morality. Remember, by 'morality', in this instance, we are seeking a theory of right action i.e., we are searching for a basic norm that is a characteristic feature of all right and/or wrong actions. One dominant interpretation of African ethics in the literature in African philosophy tends to specify harmonious or communal relationships as the defining feature of all right actions. In this interpretation morality *en toto* revolves around harmonious or communal relations. Note the following comment:

> (T)here was another value being pursued, namely the establishing and maintaining of harmonious relationships. Again and again in discussion and in general conversation this stood out *as a desired and enjoyed end in itself*, often as the ultimate rationale for action (Silberbauer 1991: 20, emphasis mine).

This quotation highlights two related aspects of value in relation to the status of harmonious relationships. On the one hand, you get the sense that they embody the kinds of relationships that are desirable and these social relations are desirable as an end. One could read the suggestion that harmonious relationships are both intrinsically valuable and serve as the proper goal of morality. To be engaged in morality involves having an attitude that highly esteems harmonious relationships, but also pursues such relationships for their own sake.

For another useful comment on the status of harmonious relationships, consider Desmond Tutu's (1999: 35) observation:

I am human because I belong.' I participate, I share... Harmony, friendliness, community are great goods. Social harmony is for us the *summum bonum* - the greatest good. Anything that subverts or undermines this sought-after good is to be avoided like the plague.

Tutu, unequivocally informs us that social harmony is the greatest good, which I understand to mean that these kinds of relations are to be prized and pursued for their own sake. Or, consider, the following comment by Metz (2010: 84, emphasis mine) grounding a moral theory on social relationships:

Note that apparently for Mbiti, Biko, Tutu, and several others who have reflected on African morality, *harmonious or communal relationships are valued for their own sake*, not merely as a means to some other basic value such as pleasure.

Following the lead of scholars of African moral thought, Mbiti, Biko and Tutu, among others, Metz posits social harmony as the highest moral good or a final good i.e., the kind of a good that ought to be valued and pursued for its own sake. For us to arrive at a robust principle of right action, we need to have a precise sense of what constitutes harmonious relationships in African thought. Metz proposes that we construe harmony to consist of two sorts social relationships: social identity and solidarity (or, good will). He makes this comment regarding identity and solidarity:

On the one hand, there is a relationship of identity, a matter of considering oneself a part of the group, experiencing life as bound up with others, being close and feeling integrated. On the other hand, there is reference to a relationship of solidarity, being committed to the good of others, aiding them, acting consequent to sympathy and being concerned for others' welfare (2014: 149).

These are two distinct kinds of social relationships. The social relationship of identity involves three aspects. Firstly, it speaks to the question of personal identity or awareness. On this view, the individual conceives of her own identity as already and always connected with others. When one refers to herself, she always thinks of herself in terms of 'we' (the relationship she shares with others) and never merely as an 'I'. The relationship of identity is a kind that is reciprocal in nature insofar as the group or others with whom a self identifies with must also identify with her and recognize her as being a part of them. The second component of identity refers to certain ideals and goals that are shared in common. That is, not only do individuals in this social relationship share a common identity, but they also share common goals and aspirations. The final component of identity involves a collaborative attitude and behaviour, where joint effort is a hallmark of pursuing tasks, goals and responsibilities shared in common (see Metz 2007a, 2014, 2021).

On the other hand, roughly, the relationship of solidarity involves an attitude and conduct grounded on goodwill, where the agent seeks to promote or secure the welfare of others for their own sakes. At the heart of solidarity is the idea of service towards others. Metz (2021: 148) informs us that –"Acting in solidarity means not merely striving to make people better off or to advance their self-interest, but also to make others better people or to advance their self-realization". The kind of service

2.3 Community and Human Dignity

we dispense to others, in terms of solidarity goes beyond merely meeting others' needs or improving their quality of life. It also, in part, and, so far as possible, aims to create conditions where people can be better (in terms of their humanity or humanness).

In sum, the social relationship of identity can be construed as one where an individual "shares a way of life" and/or "identifies with others" insofar as she belongs and reaps the benefits and burdens of common membership in a group (Metz 2021: 146 & 144). The relationship of solidarity, on the other hand, is one where the agent regards and treats the moral patient as an object of service. The service associated with solidarity is one that is characterized by care, which is motivated by moral emotions of empathy and sympathy. The goal of the service associated with solidarity involves, at the very least, securing the welfare of the moral patient, and, at most, the creation of enabling conditions for agents to be able to pursue a decent human existence.

The perfect example of the social relationship of identity is exemplified by a soccer team. Take Barcelona, for example. All the players define themselves as members of the Barcelona family. They play together as a team to achieve the common goal of winning. Even though there are players that display individual brilliance and it is individuals that score goals. It is the team as a whole that wins. An example of the relationship of solidarity is sending aid to some distraught strangers in a foreign country. Metz, in relation to these two kinds of social relationships, makes an interesting observation. He notes that you can have one kind of relationship without another. He gives an example of a typical capitalist firm like Amazon. Though employees and the management have a relationship of identity since they all are all members of the Amazon family, this relationship is usually fraught with tensions as these two groups tend to have perennial labour disputes surrounding remuneration, among others (see Metz 2007a, 2015). One group offers what they consider to be competitive remuneration, but another tends to believe that they deserve more.

In Metz's view, the best way to represent harmony is by combining these two social relationships. He captures the essence of his moral theory in this fashion:

> The combination of the relationships of identity and solidarity, or of sharing a way of life with others and caring for their quality of life, is basically what English speakers mean by 'friendliness' or 'love' in a broad sense. Hence, one can sum up one major swathe of traditional African thought about how to live by saying that one's highest-order end should be to live a genuinely human way of life, which one must do by prizing harmonious or friendly relationships (Metz 2014: 149).

The defining essence of harmonious relationships is that they are characterized by "friendliness" or "love" (Metz 2009: 52; 2021: 154). Friendliness is a kind of virtue that requires some kind of social contact in the first place. It is crucial to appreciate, however, that for Metz (2021: 153) it is better to construe the idea of friendliness in African thought in a way that "connotes less emotional intensity". The moral-theoretical content and focus of friendliness is on "a sense of togetherness, cooperative interaction, aid, and sympathetic altruism". The same logic attends to the value of love. On the one hand, it appreciates that there is a relationship (of identity) between the lover and the beloved, and it also understands this relation to be one where there is reciprocal care, which involves actively responding to the needs, welfare of others, and the general conditions for thriving as a human being.

We are now in a position to express Metz's principle of right action. Right actions are definable essentially in terms of harmonious relationships. Metz (2009: 51) expresses this principle as follows:

> ... an action is right just insofar as it is a way of living harmoniously or prizing communal relationships, ones in which people identify with each other and exhibit solidarity with one another; otherwise, an action is wrong.

Right actions are characterized by the feature of prizing harmonious relationships and, wrongs ones, on the other hand, have the opposite effect of sowing hate and divisions. Two further important considerations should be borne in mind in relation to this principle of right action. On the one hand, we might ask the question – how ought we to relate to the value of harmony, is it the kind that we *promote* or one that we *honour*? This question expressed in simple terms is about whether this principle takes a consequentialist or deontological form. In the first statement of this principle, Metz (2007a: 338 emphasis mine) used a consequentialist language that required the agent to "*promote* shared identity among people grounded on good-will". Notice, however, in the quotation I cited to express Metz's principle of right action, he uses the language of *prizing* harmonious relationships since he is now committed to the view that a plausible rendition of African moral thought ought to take a deontological posture. The implication of "a deontological interpretation" is that the agent is required to merely respect harmonious living even if doing so might have negative consequences (Metz 2021: 163). As opposed to a consequentialist rendition that requires the production of as much as possible harmony even if it might require one to employ disharmonious means (see MacNaughton and Rawling 1992).

The second consideration related to this principle of right action is that it is, to some degree, characterized by moral partialism. 'Moral partialism' is the claim that morality, at least to some extent, ought to accommodate special relationships and their attended special obligations. Metz (2014: 149) comments in this fashion regarding partiality in relation to this principle:

> One's own harmonious or friendly relationships matter most for typical African approaches to morality; 'family first' and 'charity begins at home' are commonly expressed, in order to indicate a principled priority going to actual ties of which one is a part.

The implication of this principle is that, all things being equal, my extant relationships ought to take priority over new ones (see Molefe 2021). In other words, I have a stronger duty to my family than to a stranger.

Above we considered Metz's normative theory, which accounts for right actions in terms of prizing harmonious relations – and it accounts for harmonious relations by appeal to sharing a way of life (social identity) and solidary (caring for others' quality of life). In this view, rape, deceit, abduction, extortion and so on are wrong because they do not involve sharing a way of life (where there is a sense of 'we', in terms of participation, consent, and so on, between the parties) and it is not attended by goodwill (where there is a thought, desire and effort to improve another's quality of life attended by general conditions for a flourishing humanity). Now, we proceed to consider a theory of human dignity associated with Metz's moral philosophy.

2.3 Community and Human Dignity

2.3.2 Metz's Theory of Human Dignity

In several places, Metz has advanced and defended a relational theory of human dignity (see Metz 2010, 2011, 2012a, b, 2017, 2021). Metz informs us that his theory of dignity is communal or relational. What does he mean by classifying it as *relational*? Metz (2012a, 2021) observes that a theory of moral status or human dignity can take the form of *individualism, holism* or *relationalism*. 'Individualistic' theories of human dignity account for it in virtue of some feature internal to the individual like a soul, rationality and so on. 'Holistic' theories for human dignity account for it on the basis of mere membership in the group without regard to individual features. 'Relationalism', on Metz's (2012a: 390) view, is a position between individualism and holism. He makes this comment to clarify relationalism: "A relational theory implies that a being warrants moral consideration only if, and because, it exhibits some kind of intensional or causal property with regard to another being". That is, a relational view of human dignity is one that is grounded on an interactive property of the individual.

Unlike an individualistic account of human dignity that merely requires the possession of an internal property to account for human dignity, a relational account insists that the capacity that does the job ought to be the kind that is essentially oriented to connect with others in certain ways. Unlike a holistic account that merely focuses on group membership, a relational account insists that the individual capacity to relate to others does the job of securing human dignity. In other words, a human being that lacks the capacity to relate with others though she is a member of the human group, on a relational view, does not have human dignity since she lacks the requisite relationship forming capacity. Now, I turn to consider Metz's relational theory of human dignity – its content.

Metz's ethical theory is relational insofar as it is grounded on harmonious relationships as the defining feature of morality. Remember that in normative theorisation, we seek to identify a basic norm that is a defining feature of all permissible actions. When theorizing about human dignity, however, we seek to identify a feature or capacity of human nature in virtue of which we can account for intrinsic human worth (Waldron 2013: 8). On his part, Metz (2010: 94) accounts for human dignity in terms of "our capacity to engage in harmonious relationships". What is the most distinctive feature that marks out human beings as morally precious and superior to the animal and vegetal kingdom is their capacity to participate in communal or harmonious relationships (Metz 2021). To get a better handle of this relational account of human dignity, I need to throw in some technical details.

Firstly, it is the possession of the *capacity* for harmonious relationships that accounts for human dignity. In other words, any entity that possesses the capacity for harmonious relationships has dignity. I emphasize that it is not the actual participation in social relationships of identity and solidarity that accounts for our status of human dignity. To capture this insight, Metz (2017) describes his account in terms of *modal relationalism*. The implication of capturing this account of human dignity in terms of *modal* relationalism is to point out that the mere possibility to participate and/or even benefit from harmonious relationships is a sufficient ground to secure human dignity. In other words, an individual that has temporarily compromised her capacity to participate in communal relationships through wanton drunkenness still has human dignity. This temporary circumstance that limits one's ability to participate in social relationships is not so radical as to ultimately alter her nature. Metz refers to such situations where one's relational abilities are temporarily limited as "contingent obstacles" or "inabilities" (Metz 2012a, b: 394; 2021: 164). This is the case because, in principle, her human nature that possesses the relevant capacity is still intact i.e., in a possible world she can still exercise the relevant capacity. The same logic applies to us when we are sleeping or in a temporary coma, our dignity is still intact, hence, still deserving utmost moral respect.

Furthermore, Metz's relational view of human dignity offers its own account of the distinction between merely having moral status, as partial or lower moral status, from full moral status, or human dignity. In Metz view, only entities that can both be *subjects* and *objects* of harmonious relationships have full moral status or human dignity. An entity is a *subject* of harmonious relationships insofar as it can initiate and participate in such relationships of friendliness *qua* identity and solidarity. An entity is an *object* of such a relationship if it can be affected by social relationships of identity and solidarity. In other words, all entities that can be beneficiaries of the relationships of friendliness, be it in terms of catering for their needs and welfare, are objects of such relationships. In his view, Metz believes that (normal adult) human beings, are the paradigm examples of an entity that stands out as both a subject and object of harmonious relationships, and have dignity. Those entities that can stand only as objects of harmonious relationships have partial moral status. Majority of animals, on Metz's view, are examples of entities that stand as objects of harmonious relationships, hence they have partial moral status.

Above, our exposition revealed that Metz accounts for African ethics in terms of certain kinds of interpersonal relationships. He accounts for right actions in terms of prizing or living harmoniously with others and wrong ones tend to breed divisions and ill-will. He explains the content of harmonious relations in terms of sharing a way of life and improving others' quality of life. Importantly, we noted that Metz advances a relational account of human dignity that accounts for it by appeal to the capacity for harmonious relationships. Only entities that can both be subjects and objects of harmonious relationships have dignity. Below, I consider personhood as the basis for human dignity.

2.4 Personhood and Human Dignity

In this section, I consider personhood-based accounts of human dignity. I consider two competing interpretations of it. One interpretation is associated with Polycarp Ikuenobe and another with Motsamai Molefe. Both these scholars specialize, among others, on the notion of personhood in the African tradition of philosophy. I will start with a general discussion of personhood as a moral perspective and I will subsequently proceed to consider the two competing views of human dignity associated with it. The notion of personhood is among the most influential in the tradition of African philosophy. The concept of personhood can be identified as among the most important in African cultures to capture an African moral *weltanschauung*. In philosophy, Ifeanyi Menkiti, a Nigerian philosopher, was the first one to give a philosophical analysis of the African traditional concept of personhood (see Menkiti 1984). Wiredu (2004: 17) makes this observation:

> In Contemporary African philosophy the *locus classicus* of the normative conception of a person is Ifeanyi Menkiti's 'Person and Community African Traditional Thought'... My own views are in substantial agreement with Menkiti's ... Personhood ... is something of an achievement.

Notice, Wiredu begins by corroborating the claim that Menkiti was the first one to subject the idea of personhood to formal philosophical analysis. Wiredu, interestingly, proceeds to shed light on the specific nature of the concept of personhood central in Menkiti's and in African philosophy in general as the normative notion of personhood. In fact, Menkiti (2004) in the restatement of his views on the traditional notion of personhood, titles his essay *On the Normative Conception of a Person*. At this point, it is important that we be clear regarding the notion of personhood in African philosophy, so we can appreciate the centrality of the normative concept of it.

2.4.1 The Notions of Personhood in African Philosophy

Scholars draw a distinction between the ontological and normative notions of personhood (Oyowe 2014). Even with regards to the ontological notion of personhood, there can be an ambiguity. To avoid this ambiguity, we may need to distinguish between the ontological notion *qua* the fact of being human and the ontological notion *qua* personal identity. The first ontological notion concerns the fact that one of the items that constitute the furniture of the world are things like you and me, the reader of this book, human beings. As much as one can identify trees, grains of sand, tables and so on, one of the things she will also identify are human beings. Moreover, the ontological status of being human is also open to philosophical scrutiny. At this level of philosophical investigation, we might be asking questions about human nature i.e. an inquiry about the kinds of properties that constitute human nature. Some interpretations of it, consider it to be entirely material and some views of it take it to be a combination of both the material and spiritual (see Gyekye 1995; Kaphagawani 2004; Wiredu 2009).

The other ontological notion revolves around the question of how to account for personal identity. The central question here is what descriptive factors constitute or explain "the idea of an individual aware of itself over time" (Metz 2013: 12). In the Western tradition, individualistic metaphysical properties like consciousness, memory, soul and so on have been proposed to provide an explanatory basis for personal identity (see Noonan 2019). In the African tradition, the standard answer invokes the community, partially or entirely, as the basis for personal identity (Menkiti 1984; Eze 2008). Another useful way to approach this debate, in light of the debates between liberals and communitarians, is in terms of *shared relations*, where the former accounts for personal identity in terms of contingently shared relations and the latter invokes essentially shared relations (see Neal and Patrick 1990).[3] I hope the reader can appreciate these two distinct ontological notions (Molefe 2019).

It is not the ontological notion, in either form, however, that tends to be the focus of African thought. Rather, the focus, as indicated by Wiredu above, tends to be on the normative notion of personhood. Before we can be precise about the content of the normative notion, we must also be aware that this notion is also attended by ambiguity. This ambiguity, in my view, is best disambiguated in the essay by Kevin Behrens (2013) *The Two "Normative" Notions of Personhood*. The first normative notion is *patient-centred* and another is *agent-centred*. The patient-centred notion assigns value to some entity by virtue of its possessing certain ontological features. The patient-centred notion of personhood, according to Behrens, is dominant in Western bioethical discourses, as it is predominantly useful in debates on issues such as abortion, euthanasia and so on. This notion is equivalent to the idea of moral status or human dignity. To claim that some entity is a person, in this sense, is tantamount to recognizing it as an object whose interests matter in their own right and ought to be duly considered in our moral decisions and actions (DeGrazia 2008).

On the other hand, Behrens informs us that the agent-centred notion of personhood is salient in the African tradition of philosophy. The view that the agent-centred notion of personhood is salient in the African tradition is endorsed by a score of scholars of African thought. Notice this comment by Gyekye (1997: 64):

> With all this said, however, this aspect of this (Menkiti's) account adumbrates a moral conception of personhood and is, on that score, interesting and relevant to the notion of personhood important for the communitarian framework.

For another consider that Wiredu (2009: 13) distinguishes between the ontological and normative concept of personhood, and he goes on to observe that interest in the latter "are more dominant" in African philosophy. Dismas Masolo (2010: 135) considers this notion to be the "pinnacle of an African difference in philosophical theory". I understand this to mean that this notion offers one of the most useful ways to gain entrance to African moral thought. Behrens (2013: 104), on his part, observes that personhood occupies a "central place ... in African philosophy". Ikuenobe (2006: 128) avers that the normative notion of personhood is the "the core of African cultural traditions".

---

[3] A contingently shared relation is a weak kind of relation, which, in one view, relationships are important but they do not "penetrate the identity of the separate selves to the point that the identity of each becomes partially or wholly constituted by the relation" (Neale and Paris 1990: 425). An essentially shared relation is one where two or more selves "each becomes partially or wholly constituted by the relation" (ibid.).

Now that we have the sense that the normative notion of personhood *qua* the agent-centred is salient in the tradition of philosophy, we can proceed to unfold it as a moral theory.

2.4.2 Personhood as a Moral Theory

To unfold personhood as a moral theory, I will consider three aspects of it. The first thing to notice about the normative notion of personhood is that it represents the final good. In other words, personhood specifies the moral goal that we (as moral agents) ought to pursue and achieve for its own sake. When we are born, we are merely human, and the goal of morality, in light of this ethical view, requires that we transcend our biological status and add to it dimensions of moral value. It is in this light that African scholars insist that personhood is some kind of moral achievement. On this understanding of personhood, it is something that we ought to pursue for its own sake.

The second question we may ask concerns the content of personhood. When we say that some agent has achieved personhood, what exactly has she achieved? The answer to this question is answered by appeal to the notion of virtue or moral excellence. The reader will notice that Menkiti closely associates or even defines personhood in terms of moral excellence. In one instance, Menkiti (1984: 172) makes the following comment –

> We must also conceive of this organism as going through a long process of social and ritual transformation until it attains the full complement of excellencies seen as truly definitive of man.

In the same essay, he observes:

> ... the African emphasized the rituals of incorporation and the overarching necessity of learning the social rules by which the community lives, so that what was initially biologically given can come to attain social self-hood, i.e., become a person with all the inbuilt excellencies implied by the term.

We can pick out several insights from these quotations. We notice that personhood is not an event, but it is an ongoing process of personal transformation that involves internalising socio-moral rules constitutive of moral excellence into one's character. In this light, personhood comes in degrees, one can be more or less of a person, and one can be declared to have no personhood at all (though they still remain human). A successful acquisition of these rules amounts to having a humanity inbuilt with excellences. At the heart of the moral concept of personhood is a journey from mere biological existence to a moral existence i.e., an existence characterized by moral excellence. To have personhood is equivalent to being an embodiment of moral excellence, which means that one has developed a virtuous character. Gyekye (1992: 110) associates personhood with the "pursuit or practice of moral virtue". In another place, Gyekye (2010) informs us that "Used normatively, the judgment, 'he is a person,' means 'he has a good character'". Wiredu (2009: 15) also tells us "that to be called a person is to be commended". In the same essay, he observes that the status of personhood is conferred to "a morally sound adult who has demonstrated in practice a sense of responsibility to household, lineage and society at large" (ibid.). In sum, to be called a person is tantamount to being recognized to be leading a morally virtuous life, which is a positive assessment of one's deportment and character.

The third aspect of personhood as a moral theory requires us to be specific and exact about the approach it takes to ethical theory. Notice these illuminating comments from the following scholars about the approach characteristic of personhood as a moral theory. Wiredu (2009: 15) observes that if the notion of personhood entails a positive assessment of one's character, it should follow that it "presupposes a system of values." Otherwise, what would be the basis for commending or criticizing the agent's conduct or character? The important task then becomes the explication of the nature of this system of values. Metz's (2007a: 331–332) takes a moral view associated with personhood to be one that requires the agent to develop "one's distinctively human and valuable nature [to embody] a self-realization ethic". Jason Van Niekerk (2007) interprets such a system of values along the lines of *auto-centrism*, which entails that the agent's primary duty is the development of her character. In a similar vein, Behrens (2013: 111) associates personhood with a perfectionist system of values:

> Menkiti's association of the term 'excellencies' with personhood also implies that becoming a person is essentially related to developing virtue. Thus, the African conception of personhood could be thought to propose a theory of ethics that brings to mind what Western philosophy calls 'perfectionism: Persons should seek to develop a good or virtuous nature in order to become true or fully moral persons.

The notion of personhood embodies a moral system centrally focused on the agent pursuing or realizing a particular ideal state in relation to improving her own humanity. In this light, it is apropos to describe it as a self-realization or perfectionist approach to ethics. Talk of self-realization insofar as it essentially enjoins the agent to morally improve her own character strikes me as tantamount to the doctrine of moral perfectionism since it involves "the development of human nature" (Wall 2012: n.p.). In sum, we observe that the normative notion of personhood embodies a perfectionist moral system, which requires the moral agent to perfect her own character, i.e. it prescribes that the agent ought to develop a virtuous character.

Before turning to the two accounts of human dignity associated with the normative concept of personhood, I discuss two important aspects associated with this moral view. Until now, I have associated personhood with moral perfection or excellence, which I understand to refer to a virtuous character. I have not yet, however, given the reader a sense of the kinds of virtues that tend to be associated with personhood. A careful analysis will reveal that personhood tends to be associated with *relational* virtues (see Metz 2012c; Molefe 2019). These are the kinds of virtues one can only develop in the context of positively interacting with others.

Tutu (1999: 31) associates personhood with being "*generous*, you are *hospitable*, you are *friendly* and *caring* and *compassionate*. You share what you have. It is to say, 'My humanity is caught up, is inextricably bound up in yours'". Gyekye (1992: 110) observes that personhood is associated with "moral virtues that can be said to include generosity, kindness, compassion, benevolence, respect and concern for others". To say that personhood is essentially characterized by relational virtues simply means those exuding with it abound with other-regarding duties.

The relational nature of the virtues associated with personhood has an implication regarding the question of means i.e. how do we attain moral perfection? The above adumbrations on the nature of virtues associated with personhood being relational imply that it can only be achieved in social relationships. Remember, Menkiti (1984: 172) informs us that personhood requires "incorporation into this or that community". He continues to observe that personhood "is attained in direct proportion as one participates in communal life through the discharge of the various obligations defined by one's station" (1984: 176). I think the point is simple, if one is expected to manifest relational virtues then it makes sense that social relationships serve as the only and best context where their development is possible and meaningful. That is, one cannot be kind, compassionate, and generous outside of the social relationships where one can learn, internalize and display these virtues.

Above, I distinguished four distinct senses of personhood in African philosophy. I went on to identify the normative notion of personhood or the agent-centred one as the one that is most salient in African philosophy. I associated the normative notion of personhood with the self-realization or perfectionist ethics, which enjoins the agent to develop a virtuous character. In light of the exposition of personhood as a moral theory, we can now turn to consider conceptions of human dignity associate with it. I begin with Ikuenobe's personhood-based account of human dignity.

2.4.3   Ikuenobe's Theory of Human Dignity

Below, I consider Ikuenobe's view of human dignity. He defends this view of human dignity in two academic essays – *The Communal Basis for Moral Dignity: An African Perspective* (2017) and *Human rights, personhood, dignity, and African communalism* (2018). By and large, at least when it comes to the view of human dignity being propounded, these essays express the same view. For that reason, in what follows, unless otherwise stated, I will draw largely from the first essay. At least, in light of how I expound Ikuenobe's view of human dignity, I suggest that it is characterized by two major features, namely: (1) it is grounded on the normative notion of personhood (that we considered above) and (2) it regards ontological capacities (like autonomy) to have instrumental value, rather than an intrinsic one. I begin by discussing the relation between personhood and human dignity.

At the heart of the moral concept of personhood, according to Ikuenobe (2017: 438), is the agent's positive moral performance characterized by "communal values of caring, mutuality, harmonious relationships, and solidarity". In the same essay, he observes that personhood is something that "is acquired, shaped, and actualized by the 'organic constitution' in, and by, a community through a process of acculturation into the values of caring and mutuality". For Ikuenobe, the moral notion of personhood, is one that is intrinsically associated with community-oriented responsibilities, where the aim is the creation of conditions for communal well-being. In this view, to have personhood means to have a character disposition armed with a truckload of other-regarding duties. To get a sense of Ikuenobe's (2017: 437) view of human dignity, we need to ascertain what he means when he states that human dignity "is founded on a moral conception of personhood"?

The answer that comes out clearly and consistently from his analysis amounts to the view that Ikuenobe equates the achievement of personhood, moral perfection, with human dignity. This reading is sustained by two considerations. On the one hand, Ikuenobe uses the two terms as if they are interchangeable. Notice this expression –"This is a significant basis for the morality of ascribing or denying personhood or dignity, and then respect by others" (2017: 446). The suggestion here seems to be that to ascribe personhood to some moral agent is the same as ascribing human dignity to them. On the same page, he appears to equate the expression that "one is not a person" with the expression "one has no moral dignity" (ibid). The first quotation above, took a positive form, here we just encountered its equivalent in a negative form, i.e. to deny one personhood is the same as denying her human dignity. This tendency of speaking of personhood and human dignity interchangeably is pervasive in the entire essay (see also 2017: 446; 448, 452–453).

On the other hand, the notion of human dignity, exactly like that of personhood, is explained in terms of moral performance and achievement. Notice this comment by Ikuenobe (2017: 438):

> Dignity involves the capacity for, and manifestation of, self-respect and respect for, and responsibility to, others. This involves how one comports oneself in one's behavior to enhance harmonious living, which implies *being worthy of respect* that engenders respect by others.

For another, consider this comment: "a plausible view of dignity must give credence to the ethical or justice perspective, which suggests that respect or entitlements *must be earned or deserved by actions*" (2017: 442 emphasis mine). In keeping with associating human dignity with desert and achievement, he favors an approach that "link(s) dignity to communal responsibility" (ibid). Human Dignity, for Ikuenobe, is the kind of a status that "arises from fulfilling these obligations, typically involving acknowledgment by others" (443). Ikuenobe (2017: 453) also informs us that a "plausible African view of dignity that involves earned respect by others based on a person's actions and proper use of his capacity for communal harmonious living". The above quotations, I believe, settle the reading that according to Ikuenobe, just like personhood, human dignity is a status that one acquires or comes to earn or deserve relative to the quality of their moral performance in relation to their duties and responsibilities to contribute to the good of all.

2.4 Personhood and Human Dignity

I now turn to the aspect of the nature and role of our ontological capacities, like autonomy, in accounting for human dignity in Ikuenobe's view of human dignity.[4] It is important to note that Ikuenobe does recognize the relevance and importance of ontological capacities in a robust conception of human dignity. This appreciation emerges in the fact that he regards both the notion of personhood and human dignity, which in my view are interchangeable notions for him, as *thick concepts*. Human dignity is a 'thick concept' insofar as it has both the descriptive and normative or evaluative aspects (see 441). Note this comment about the descriptive component of personhood or human dignity

> ... the individual has the rational and cognitive capacities for agency and free choice. These capacities involve the ability to learn, internalize, and act in ways that promote communalism and its values of caring, mutuality, solidarity, positive identity, harmonious relationships, well-being, and dignity (2017: 447).

One thing is clear. Without these capacities, at least in their developed state, there would be no meaningful basis to expect individuals to care for one another, build harmonious relationships and promote communal well-being. In this sense, these human capacities, in a sense, are crucial and are worth taking seriously. What is worth noting, however, about Ikuenobe's view of these capacities is that he considers them to be merely instrumental. It is necessary for human dignity to have the capacities, but these capacities are not sufficient for a plausible view of it. On this view, human dignity requires more than just the mere possession of the capacities. Ikuenobe (2017: 461) expresses this view as follows:

> In this regard, it is my view that human capacities are only an instrumental good; they are only means for good life, choices, and actions that manifest respect for self and others, caring, mutuality and harmonious relationships.

To possess certain ontological capacities simply means one can, or even ought to, develop them. These capacities, however, in and of themselves, have no intrinsic value. In other words, all things being equal, the mere possession of capacities does not secure or warrant any kind of moral recognition or respect. Respect associated with capacities must emerge only in contexts where one has consistently developed and used them positively for the benefit of the moral community.

In sum, we note that Ikuenobe equates the achievement of personhood with human dignity. In his view, human dignity is not an inherent feature that one has by merely being born human. It is a kind of achievement associated with positively contributing to the welfare of society. At the heart of this notion of human dignity is the development of one's capacities, whose development is a function of caring and exercising communal responsibilities for the sake of promoting communal welfare. In this sense, to have dignity is to be recognized and praised as a moral exemplar, for developing a character that is exuding with other-regarding duties.

I turn now to Molefe's account of human dignity.

---

[4]The reader should keep in mind that Ikuenobe (2015) subscribes to a relational conception of autonomy, which understands autonomy to be an emergent of our communal practices.

2.4.4 Molefe's Theory of Human Dignity

Molefe develops his view of human dignity in three places. In the first instance, he suggests his own view of human dignity by offering a critical analysis of Ikuenobe's view of it (see Molefe 2019: Ch.5). He also articulates this view when he considers various themes in applied ethics like that of the equality of women and the place of animals in the moral community (Molefe 2020a). Finally, he develops this idea in the context of African bioethics, where he considers the status of abortion and euthanasia (in terms of their permissibility) in light of African moral thought (Molefe 2020b). For Molefe, the notion of personhood, at least, embodies two essentially connected aspects of ethical theory – the patient-centred and agent-centred dimensions of it. The patient-centred and agent-centred dimensions represent different sides of the same moral coin associated with what he calls "the ethics of personhood" (Molefe 2020c: 194). Notice here, the discussion is not merely about the normative notion of personhood, which is tantamount to the agent-centred notion of personhood.

In Molefe's view, the agent-centred notion of personhood is the final good i.e., the chief goal of morality (see Molefe 2020c). The patient-centred aspect of personhood refers to that metaphysical feature of human nature that makes the pursuit and achievement of personhood possible in the first place. In this light, talk of the patient-centred notion is tantamount to the moral idea of moral status or human dignity. Remember, Behrens (2013) does draw the distinction between the patient-centered and agent-centered notions of personhood, but associates the former with Western and the latter with the African tradition. In Molefe's view, a robust interpretation of African ethical theory ought surely to have a metaphysical basis for believing that human beings can achieve personhood (moral excellence) – I will say more on this aspect when I adumbrate Molefe's view of human dignity *qua* the patient-centred notion. Molefe's view also differs from Ikuenobe's view in that he considers the metaphysical capacities that ground the possibility for moral perfection to be intrinsically valuable rather than merely instrumental. That is, in Molefe's view, the mere possession of these capacities is sufficient ground for human dignity without the requirement of any moral performance.

We can now proceed to consider how Molefe accounts for the metaphysical stuff that accounts for human dignity *qua* the patient-centred notion of personhood. Molefe draws from the intellectual resources provided by two leading scholars of personhood, Menkiti and Gyekye. The point is not that these scholars do actually associate the normative notion of personhood with a particular view of human dignity. Rather, Molefe's argument is that a particular view of human dignity can be extracted from their adumbrations on the normative concept of personhood without suggesting that this is their own view or that they would even agree with it (see Molefe 2020b). Molefe, at the very least, assumes that his interpretation of their ideas does not mar their original views on the normative notion of personhood, instead, it offers one way to extend their moral views.

2.4 Personhood and Human Dignity

To extract the concept of human dignity from Menkiti's adumbrations, Molefe notices that the notion of justice features in Menkiti's exposition of personhood. The notion of justice features insofar as Menkiti (1984: 176) believes that John Rawls "comes closest to a recognition of this importance of ethical sense in the definition of personhood". The concept of personhood, in this context, is directly associated with justice (ibid). It is interesting to notice that the ethical notion invoked here is distinct from the agent-centred one (which is central in Menkiti's exposition), but here we are dealing with a patient-centred one. According to Molefe, three considerations support the claim that the focus in this passage is on the patient-centred notion.

Firstly, as quoted by Menkiti (1984: 177, emphasis mine), Rawls informs us that "The sufficient condition for equal justice [is] the *capacity* for moral personality". Menkiti affirms this reading of Rawls by insisting that "individuals comes to deserve the duties of justice . . . only through possession of a capacity for moral personality" (ibid, emphasis mine). The moral notion of personhood under consideration is a capacity-based based one as opposed to one that is "attained in direct proportion as one participates in communal life through the discharge of the various obligation" (ibid). It is some capacity that does the job in this context. Secondly, this notion of personhood is relevant in the discourse of equal justice or egalitarianism. The patient-centred notion, as a capacity-based concept, is more apt to secure egalitarianism than a performance-based notion. On a capacity-based notion, we respect the moral patient for no other reason other than the mere possession of the relevant capacity, and any entity that possesses such a capacity is owed equal regard[5] (see Molefe 2021). Whereas a performance-based notion of personhood is overtly inegalitarian since performance is a differential and differentiating property.

The final reason why this notion of a person is patient-centred is that he connects it with rights, and rights generally tend to operate on accounts that are capacity-based based on personhood (Freeman 1995). Menkiti (1984: 177) also seems to follow this tendency in moral philosophy. Consider this comment:

> . . . persons are the sort of entities that are owed the duties of justice, it must also be allowed that each time we find an ascription of any of the various rights implied by these duties of justice, the conclusion naturally follows that the possessor of the rights in question cannot be other than a person. That is so because the basis of such rights ascription has now been made dependent on a possession of a capacity for moral sense, a capacity, which though it need not be realized (ibid.).

In Menkiti's view, rights are owed to persons. 'Persons', in this context, refers to those entities with the capacity for moral sense – a patient-centred notion. Again, Menkiti is unequivocal that the notion of personhood is a capacity-based one, and he is very specific about the capacity that secures equal justice, which is expressed through equal rights – the capacity for moral sense.

---

[5] I admit that we may not have the same capacities, but this consideration is quite beside the point. The point is we are evaluating the standing of entities merely on possessing the capacity or not, and if one possesses it, they are equal to any other entity that possesses it.

In light of this rough analysis of Menkiti's moral philosophy, Molefe believes that Menkiti may be construed to hold a moral philosophy that is characterized by both the patient-centred and agent-centred notions of personhood. The patient-centred notion embodies Menkiti's view of human dignity in virtue of which human beings deserve equal respect or even human rights. It is also this capacity for moral sense that explains why we ought to expect human beings to be able to pursue and achieve moral excellence (agent-centred notion of personhood) in the first place.

In his analysis, Molefe (2020a) also picks out the same moral logic of the patient-and-agent-centred aspects of value theory associated with the notion of personhood in Gyekye's exposition of personhood. Molefe notices that Gyekye's exposition of personhood moves from an extensive analysis of the agent-centred notion of personhood that it is undergirded by its own conception of human dignity (a patient-centred theory of value). Gyekye (1992: 111) makes the following comment that, in Molefe's view, directly connects that patient-and-agent-centred views of personhood:

> The foregoing discussion of some morally significant expressions in the Akan language or judgements made about the conduct of persons suggests a conception of moral personhood; a person is defined in terms of *moral qualities or capacities*: a human person is a being who has a *moral sense* and is *capable of making moral judgments*.

Note here, Gyekye seems to be arguing that the agent-centred notion of personhood suggests a conception of human dignity (or, what Gyekye calls *moral personhood*). Also notice that moral personhood is defined in terms of moral capacities, which Gyekye explains in terms of being endowed with moral sense or capability to make moral judgements. Like Menkiti, Gyekye assigns intrinsic value to human beings in virtue of their possessing the capacity for moral sense. Gyekye (1992: 110) also refers to this capacity for moral sense as the "capacity for virtue". The capacity for virtue refers to the agent's complex psychological capacities to make moral judgements, which endowments are essential to pursue and attain moral excellence.

In this light, Molefe takes the normative notions quite seriously in his moral philosophy. His argument is that this notion is intrinsically connected with the underlying notion of human dignity, which is accounted for by the capacity for virtue. Hence, we can expect moral agents to pursue and achieve a virtuous life precisely because they have the capacity for virtue. Molefe (2020b: 120) makes the following remark:

> What makes a human life distinctive biologically and morally, in terms of the discourse of personhood, is the possibility of pursuing moral perfection. This possibility is predicated on a certain fact of human nature, the ability or capacity for virtue ... we concluded that moral agents are able to pursue personhood because they have the capacity for virtue ... Alternatively, to express this view lucidly, the concept of personhood envisages a moral agent that [is] able to (develop) the moral capacity (for) virtue. As such, to say of some moral agent that she has achieved personhood is tantamount to the idea that she is characterised by a dignified human existence. The capacity for virtue refers to *intrinsic* or *status dignity*, and the acquisition of personhood (moral excellence) refers to *extrinsic* or *achievement dignity*.

In light of this quotation, we come to the following observations. In Molefe's view, the patient-centred notion, which is the same as a theory of human dignity, is a function of the capacity for virtue. Human beings have human dignity merely because they possess this capacity. The kind of dignity associated with the capacity for virtue is the *status dignity* (Formasa and Catriona 2014). We expect human beings to pursue and achieve human dignity because they have the capacity for virtue. The development of the capacity for virtue amounts to moral perfection or the acquisition of a virtuous character. It is *achievement dignity* that is associated with the development of the capacity for virtue (ibid.).

To conclude this section of the chapter, it might be helpful to contrast both Ikuenobe's and Molefe's view of human dignity. For Ikuenobe, capacities are merely instrumentally valuable and for Molefe capacities are intrinsically valuable. Hence, Ikuenobe does not and cannot ground human dignity on capacities since they do not have intrinsic value, and Molefe can because for him they do. Another point of contrast is that Ikuenobe locates intrinsic dignity in the actual achievement of moral excellence, whereas Molefe grounds intrinsic dignity in the capacity for virtue. In Ikuenobe's account, intrinsic dignity is associated with responsibility and desert and in Molefe's view it is a function of merely possessing the relevant capacity. In Molefe's view, the acquisition of personhood is tantamount to achievement dignity, which is distinct from intrinsic/status dignity that refers to a status of value that one has merely because they possess the relevant ontological features (Miller 2017; Formasa and Catriona 2014).

2.5 Conclusion

In this chapter, I considered three fundamental concepts, which would serve as a foundation for human dignity in the African tradition – vitality, community or harmony and personhood. In relation to vitality, I observed that it accounts for human dignity in terms of possessing vitality. The status of dignity associated with human dignity is best explained in terms of two crucial considerations. Firstly, human beings occupy a high and special place in the hierarchy. Secondly, human beings are the *image* of the three spheres of existence. In relation to Metz's relational account, it explains human dignity in terms of our capacity for harmonious relations, which harmonious relationships are explained in terms of identity and solidarity. Human beings have human dignity because they can both be subjects and objects of harmonious relationships. I distinguished two competing personhood-based views of human dignity. One reduces it to the actual achievement of moral perfection that the agent attains relative to embodying moral perfection, which manifests through a consistent exercise of care, solidarity and communal responsibilities. On the other rendition, it is accounted for by appeal to the mere possession of the capacity for virtue. The capacity for virtue, is a set of psychological abilities, required for human beings to be able to pursue moral perfection.

In the next chapter, I will apply these four theories of human dignity to the cases of euthanasia, animals and disability ethics.

References

Ashcroft, Richard (2005) Making sense of dignity. J Med Ethics 31:679–682

Asouzu I (2007) Ibuanyidanda: new complementary ontology beyond world Immanentism, ethnocentric reduction and impositions. LIT VERLAG, Zurich

Attoe A (2020) A systematic account of African conceptions of the meaning of/in life. S Afr J Philos 39:127–139

Behrens K (2013) Two 'normative' conceptions of personhood. Quest 25:103–119

Bikopo B, van Bogaert L (2009) Reflection on euthanasia: Western and African Ntomba perspectives on the death of a chief. Dev World Bioeth 10:42–48

Bujo B (2005) Differentiations in African ethics. In: Schweiker W (ed) The Blackwell companion to religious ethics. Blackwell Publishing, Oxford, pp 419–434

Bujo B (2009) Ecology and ethical responsibility from an African perspective. In: Murove F (ed) African ethics: an anthology of comparative and applied ethics. University of Kwa-Zulu Natal Press, Pietermaritzburg, pp 391–411

Chimakonam J, Ogbonnaya L (2021) African metaphysics, epistemology and a new logic. Palgrave Macmillan, Cham

DeGrazia D (2008) Moral status as a matter of degree? South J Philos 46:181–198

Donnelly J (2015) Normative versus taxonomic humanity: varieties of human dignity in the Western tradition. J Hum Rights 14:1–22

Dzobo N (1992a) Values in a changing society: man, ancestors and god. In: Wiredu K, Gyekye K (eds) Person and community: Ghanian philosophical studies. Center for Research in Values and Philosophy, Washington, pp 223–240

Dzobo K (1992b) Values in a changing society: man, ancestors and god. In: Wiredu K, Gyekye K (eds) Person and community: Ghanaian philosophical studies, 1. Council for Research in Values and Philosophy, Washington, DC, pp 223–242

Eze O (2005) Ubuntu: a communitarian response to Liberal individualism. University of Pretoria, Pretoria

Eze M (2008) What is African communitarianism? Against consensus as a regulative ideal. S Afr J Philos 27:386–399

Formasa P, Catriona M (2014) Nussbaum, Kant, and the capabilities approach to dignity. Ethical Theory Moral Pract 17:875–892

Freeman M (1995) The philosophical foundations of human rights. Hum Rights Q 16:491–514

Gamwell F (2005) Norms, values and metaphysics. In: Schweiker W (ed) The Blackwell companion to religious ethics. Blackwell Publishing, Oxford, pp 112–120

Gyekye K (1992) Person and community in African thought. In: Wiredu K, Gyekye K (eds) Person and community: Ghanaian philosophical studies, 1. Council for Research in Values and Philosophy, Washington, DC, pp 101–124

Gyekye K (1995) An essay on African philosophical thought: the Akan conceptual scheme. Temple University Press, Philadelphia

Gyekye K (1997) Tradition and modernity: philosophical reflections on the African experience. Oxford University Press, New York

Gyekye K (2010) African ethics. In: Zalta E (ed) The Stanford encyclopedia of philosophy. Available at: http://plato.stanford.edu/archives/fall2011/entries/african-ethics

Idziak J (1980) Divine command morality: historical and contemporary readings. Edwin Mellen, New York

Ikuenobe P (2015) Relational autonomy, personhood, and African traditions. Philos East West 65: 1005–1029

Ikuenobe P (2017) The communal basis for moral dignity: an African perspective. Philos Pap 45: 437–469

Ikuenobe P (2018) Human rights, personhood, dignity, and African communalism. J Hum Rights 17:589–604

References

Imafidon E (2013) On the ontological foundation of a social ethics in African traditions. In: Imafidon E, Bewaji J (eds) Ontologized ethics: new essays in African meta-ethics. Lexington Books, New York, pp 37–54

Iroegbu P (2005) Do all persons have a right to life? In: Iroegbu P, Echekwube A (eds) Kpim of morality ethics: general, special and professional. Heinamann Educational Books (Nigerial) Plc, Ibadan, pp 78–83

Jones E, Metz T (2015) The politics of doing philosophy in Africa: a conversation. S Afr J Philos 34:538–550

Kaphagawani D (2004) African conceptions of a person: a critical survey. In: Wiredu K (ed) Companion to African philosophy. Blackwell Publishing, Oxford, pp 332–442

Kittay E (2005) Equality, dignity and disability. In: Waldron A, Lyons F (eds) Perspectives on equality: the second Seamus Heaney lectures. Liffey, Dublin, pp 95–122

LenkaBula P (2008) Beyond anthropocentricity-Botho/Ubuntu and the quest for economic and ecological justice. Relig Theol 15:375–394

MacNaughton D, Rawling P (1992) Honoring and promoting values. Ethics 102:835–843

Magesa L (1997) African religion: the moral traditions of abundant life. Orbis Books, New York

Malpas J (2007) Human dignity and human beings. In: Malpas J, Lickiss N (eds) Perspectives on human dignity: a conversation. Springer, New York

Masolo D (2010) Self and community in a changing world. Indiana University Press, Indianapolis

Mbiti J (1969a) Religions and philosophy. Doubleday and Company, New York

Mbiti J (1969b) African religions and philosophy. Doubleday and Company, New York

Menkiti I (1984) Person and community in African traditional thought. In: Wright RA (ed) African philosophy: an introduction. University Press of America, Lanham, pp 171–181

Menkiti I (2004) On the normative conception of a person. In: Wiredu K (ed) Companion to African philosophy. Blackwell, Oxford, pp 324–331

Metz T (2007a) Toward an African moral theory. J Polit Philos 15:321–341

Metz T (2007b) Ubuntu as a moral theory: reply to four critics. South Afr J Philos 24:369–387

Metz T (2009) African and Western moral theories in bioethical context. Dev World Bioeth 10:49–58

Metz T (2010) Human dignity, capital punishment and an African moral theory: toward a new philosophy of human rights. J Hum Rights 9:81–99

Metz T (2011) Ubuntu as a moral theory and human rights in South Africa. Afr Hum Rights Law J 11:532–559

Metz T (2012a) An African theory of moral status: a relational alternative to individualism and holism. Ethical Theory Moral Pract: Int Forum 14:387–402

Metz T (2012b) African conceptions of human dignity: vitality and community as the ground of human rights. Hum Rights Rev 13:19–37

Metz T (2012c) Ethics in Africa and in Aristotle: some points of contrast. Phronimon Volume 13. pp 99–117

Metz T (2014) Harmonizing global ethics in the future: a proposal to add south and east to west. J Glob Ethic 10:46–155

Metz T (2015) An African egalitarianism: bringing community to bear on community. In: Hull G (ed) The equal society: essays on equality in theory and practice. Rowman & Littlefield, Lanham, pp 185–208

Metz T (2017) How to ground animal rights on African values: reply to Horsthemke. J Animal Ethics 7:163–174

Metz T (2021) A relational moral theory: African ethics in and beyond the continent. Oxford University Press, Oxford

Miller S (2017) Reconsidering dignity relationally. Ethics Soc Welf 11:108–121

Molefe M (2015a) Explorations in African meta-ethics: can a case be made for a supernaturalist position? Doctoral dissertation, University of Johannesburg, Johannesburg

Molefe M (2015b) A rejection of humanism in the African moral tradition. Theoria 63:59–77

Molefe M (2018) African metaphysics and religious ethics. Filosofia Theoretica 7:1–37

Molefe M (2019) An African philosophy of personhood, morality and politics. Palgrave Macmillan, New York

Molefe M (2020a) African personhood and applied ethics. NISC [Pty]Ltd., Grahamstown

Molefe M (2020b) An African ethics of personhood and bioethics: a reflection on abortion and euthanasia. Palgrave MacMillan, New York

Molefe M (2020c) Solving the conundrum of African philosophy through personhood: the individual or community. J Value Inq 54(1):41–57

Molefe M (2021) Partiality and impartiality in African philosophy. Lexington Books, Lanham

Neale P, Paris D (1990) Liberalism and the communitarian critique: a guide for the perplexed. Can J Polit Sci 23(3):419–439

Nel P (2008) Morality and religion in African thought. Acta Theologica 2:33–44

Nisbett RE, Peng K, Choi I, Norenzayan A (2001) Culture and systems of thought: holistic versus analytic cognition. Psychol Rev 108:291–310

Nussbaum M (2008) Human dignity and political entitlements. In: Schulman A (ed) Human dignity and bioethics: essays commissioned by the President's Council. President's Council on Bioethics, Washington, DC, pp 351–380

Nussbaum M (2011) Creating capabilities: the human development approach. The Belknap Press of Harvard University Press, Cambridge, MA

Oyowe A (2014) Fiction, culture and the concept of a person. Res Afr Lit 45:42–62

Rachels J, Rachels S (2015) The elements of moral philosophy. McGraw Hill, Boston

Rosen M (2012) Dignity: its history and meaning. Harvard University Press, Cambridge, MA

Schulman A (2008) Bioethics and the question of human dignity. In: The President's Council on bioethics, human dignity and bioethics: essays Commissioned by the President's Council. President's Council on Bioethics, Washington, DC, pp 2–19

Shutte A (2001) Ubuntu: an ethic for a new South Africa. Cluster Publications, Pietermaritzburg

Silberbauer G (1991) Ethics in small-scale societies. In: Singer P (ed) A companion to ethics. Basil Blackwell, Oxford, pp 14–28

Tempels P (1959) Bantu philosophy (C. King, Trans.). Présence Africaine, Paris

Toscano M (2011) Human dignity as high moral status. Ethics Forum 6:4–25

Tutu D (1999) No future without forgiveness. Random House, New York

Van Niekerk J (2007) In defence of an autocentric account of Ubuntu. S Afr J Philos 26:364–368

Verhoef H, Michel C (1997) Studying morality within the African context: a model of moral analysis and construction. J Moral Educ 26:389–407

Waldron J (2013) Is dignity the foundation of human rights? New York University Public Law and Legal Theory Working Papers. Paper 374. http://lsr.nellco.org/nyu_plltwp/374

Wiredu K (1996) Cultural universals and particulars: an African perspective. Indiana University Press, Indianapolis

Wiredu K (2004) Introduction: African philosophy in our time. In: Wiredu K (ed) Companion to African philosophy. Blackwell Publishing, Oxford, pp 1–27

Wiredu K (2009) An oral philosophy of personhood: comments on philosophy and orality. Res Afr Lit 40:8–18

Chapter 3
African Theories of Human Dignity: Euthanasia, Animal Ethics and Disability

Abstract This chapter applies African theories of human dignity to select themes in applied ethics. Specifically, it applies the four theories of human dignity to the cases of euthanasia, animal ethics and to people living with disabilities (severely mentally disabled individuals). In terms of euthanasia, it considers whether these four theories would permit voluntary euthanasia. On animal ethics, it considers whether these theories are anthropocentric or non-anthropocentric. In relation to disability ethics, it investigates whether the severely mentally disabled have a place in the moral community.

Keywords Anthropocentrism · Animal ethics · Applied ethics · Euthanasia · Severely mentally disabled individuals

3.1 Introduction

The focus of this chapter is on applied ethics. It is a progression from an exposition of African theories of human dignity to their application, where we consider their implications for practical problems. In this chapter, for the sake of giving the reader a deeper understanding of these theories of moral status and/or human dignity, I will apply them to the cases of euthanasia, animal ethics and disability ethics. I selected these cases, in part, because they are among those that are generally under-explored in the literature in African philosophy. In this light, they will serve as a useful foil to give us a better understanding of the theories under consideration. In relation to euthanasia, I will be inquiring if these theories would permit or forbid voluntary euthanasia. In relation to animal ethics, I will be exploring if these theories of human dignity are anthropocentric or not. Finally, in relation to disability ethics, I will be considering if these theories have a place for severely (especially mentally) disabled individuals in the moral community.

I must emphasize to the reader that the aim is not to offer a critical exposition of these four theories, where the aim is to ascertain, which, among the four, is the most promising in relation to its implications for the practical cases to be considered here. Rather, the aim is to further their exposition to give a philosophical picture, except that now, it does so in the context of applying them to the said cases. I must also

---

© The Author(s), under exclusive license to Springer Nature Switzerland AG 2022

M. Molefe, *Human Dignity in African Philosophy*, SpringerBriefs in Philosophy,

https://doi.org/10.1007/978-3-030-93217-6_3

point out to the reader that there are theories of human dignity, like that of Metz and to some extent, Molefe, where the authors associated with them, as the reader will see in this chapter, have applied them to the cases under consideration. In the case of such authors, I will draw from them as much as is possible. In the case where the theories have not been extensively applied, like in the case of vitality ethics and Ikuenobe's theory, to the cases under consideration, I will rely on my own intuition, understanding and interpretation of these theories to apply them to the cases under consideration. This chapter should be read as merely proffering one way to interpret and apply these theories of human dignity to these cases.

I structure this chapter into three major sections. Each section will deal with each of the themes in applied ethics – euthanasia, animal ethics and disability ethics – in light of the four theories. I begin below with euthanasia.

3.2 Euthanasia

This section explores the question of euthanasia in light of the African theories of human dignity. The concept of 'euthanasia' is usually defined in terms of a good death or as mercy killing (Ncayiyana 2012). Euthanasia is typically recommended in a medical context, where a terminally ill patient (under conditions of excruciating and unbearable pain) requests to be killed so as to be relieved from their suffering, particularly when there is no prospect of the pain subsiding, recovery and death is the immediate destiny (Young 2007). At least two elements are crucial to capture the essence of the concept of euthanasia. The first element is that of *intention*, where the medical practitioner knowingly and deliberately kills or lets the patient die (Wreen 1988). The second element involves the *purpose* of effecting this death; it is effected for the sole reason of benefitting the sick, suffering and dying patient, by administering death as a form of relief (Beauchamp and Davidson 1978). In this light, we note that euthanasia is a bioethical theme asking the question – "when might it be permissible for medical professionals to cause the death of human beings (medical patient) knowingly?" (Metz 2021: 280).

To properly contextualize the discussion that will follow, I urge the reader to note the following stipulations. Firstly, euthanasia is usually recommended in extreme medical situations. In this section, I stipulate that an extreme medical condition is characterized in terms of "a terminal illness" and "protracted unbearable pain with no possible medical intervention", where the patient will be dying soon (Molefe 2020a: 106). Secondly, I am aware of the distinction among *voluntary* (where a cognitively competent patient requests for it), *non-voluntary* (a case of it in a situation where the patient cannot make the request for herself due a medical condition such as being in a persistent vegetative state) and *involuntary* (where it is performed without the consent or even against the will and wish of the patient) euthanasia (Young 2007). In this section, I will limit my focus to voluntary euthanasia. I will also assume that the patient is mentally and emotionally competent to make such a request and that the decision they make is stable and enduring over time (Brock 1993).

In what follows, I consider the implications of vitality for euthanasia.

3.2.1 Vitality and Euthanasia

The central question here is whether the view of human dignity associated with vitality would permit euthanasia. I must begin by informing the reader that I am not aware of the application of vitality ethics to the bioethical problem of euthanasia.[1] Given the view of moral status (or, human dignity) associated with vitality, which accounts for it in terms of human beings possessing higher quantities of it, I think there are two possible competing interpretations of how it might address the question of euthanasia.

One possible interpretation of vitality strikes me to be comparable to that of the Catholic view of human dignity, which accounts for it in terms of the sanctity and inviolability of human life. This interpretation is possible precisely because the mere possession of vitality is understood to entail that human life is "divine in resemblance" and of "high value", and, thus, it deserves the "highest respect" (Iroegbu 2005: 448). One way to make sense of the highest respect associated with human life, given its divine status, is to consider it to be absolutely inviolable. The inviolability involved here is of a kind that strips human agents of any moral powers to make determinations about when human life should start or end, without regard to the medical condition of a person. This view, in the context of the Catholic view of human dignity, is expressed as follows:

> From the above prohibitions against suicide and abortion, and the equation of artificial means of health care with the right to basic health care, one can assume that God-given dignity makes human life sacred. If dignity forbids suicide, abortion and the removal of feeding tubes, then dignity demands respect for the sanctity of human life (Schroeder and Bani-Sadr 2017: 47).

The Catholic view accounts for the sanctity of human beings by appealing to the idea that they are created in the image of God. The vitality view accounts for the sanctity of human life by appeal to them possessing higher quantities of vitality. We might then take the sanctity of life interpretation of vitality ethics to imply that euthanasia is impermissible under all circumstances. In fact, on this view, euthanasia would amount to violating human dignity, which will make it an egregious instance of murder.

One might here accuse this rendition of vitality, which forbids euthanasia, of entailing insensitivity and lack of empathy towards the suffering and dying. On this interpretation of vitality, this accusation is not taken quite seriously because the supposed human kindness must never deviate or even oppose the divine will or jurisdiction. The standard of morality is the divine will, which places the issues

---

[1] I am aware that Bikopo and van Bogaert in the essay 'Reflection on Euthanasia: Western and African Ntomba Perspectives on the Death of a Chief'. It explores the question of euthanasia in light of the practice of hastening the death of a king for the sake of preserving the vitality of the nation. Surely, there are lessons we could learn from this practice or ritual. I personally find the practice invoked as a possible instance of euthanasia to be anachronistic and it is diametrically opposed to the ethos of human rights. Hence, I prefer a dignity-based approach to discourses of euthanasia.

pertaining to the beginning or end of life beyond the human moral and legal jurisdiction. Human agents, in the moral and legal contexts, have no right to legislate who is to live or die, whether in the case of abortion or euthanasia.

There is another interpretation of vitality, which I believe is more consistent with the intuitions dominant in African cultures in relation to euthanasia. This interpretation of vitality I believe might permit euthanasia. This interpretation of vitality ethics does also consider human life, in some sense, to be sacred. It does not, however, consider sacredness to always imply inviolability in a way that forbids all kinds of killings, particularly what might count as positive killing for the sake of relief of the very old, frail and dying. Remember that our discussion of vitality in the previous chapter distinguished between processual and absolute death. Processual death involves the state of decline of one's vitality, which is generally a bad thing, morally speaking, since the essence of morality is to grow or intensify vitality. We could here distinguish between a biological and moral processual death. A moral kind of processual death is when one's vitality is waning due to her own agency or conduct in the moral theatre. A biological processual death is when one's state of health debilitates and depreciates largely due to natural conditions (like having a cancer or some terrible accident). Usually, there is a causal relationship between the moral and biological in this moral scheme, when one's failure in the moral manifests in the biological or even natural or social, where one either is attacked by some biological disease or disability, or one's family or wealth is negatively affected (Shutte 2001; Bujo 2009).

In a context where one's medical condition, due to biological deterioration, is seriously compromised – where they are a victim of a terminal disease and live under unbearable conditions of suffering – the vitality ethic might permit euthanasia. The underlying moral logic is that one has reached a state where they can no longer participate in the struggle against (moral) death, understood normatively to refer to a state where one's vitality is declining due to an extremely bad health (or, moral) condition. Remember, the moral purpose of our existence just is to overcome moral death and to have our lives flourish by way of intensifying vitality. Should we, however, get to a point where we can no longer engage in this battle against death for reasons of our medical condition, we have now entered the zone where euthanasia is permissible. On this rendition, inviolability is conditional upon our biological and moral condition to engage in the moral battle to intensify our own vitality.[2] If our medical condition has deteriorated to a level where we can no longer engage in this moral fight against death, voluntary euthanasia is permissible.[3]

---

[2] I wish to suggest that I do not believe that this implies that those who have reached an extreme medical condition due to their moral failure do not qualify for euthanasia. This would be a wrong conclusion. The deciding factor is whether one still possess the capacity to grow their vitality or not.

[3] It occurs to me that this interpretation of vitality ethics that permits voluntary euthanasia might also endorse non-voluntary and involuntary euthanasia. I say so because the moral basis for the permissibility of euthanasia is whether an individual has objectively reached a state where they can no longer engage in the moral fight against death, and they also can no longer grow their vitality. It seems that for any individual, that has reached such a medical state, whether they can give consent

3.2 Euthanasia 51

Above, we noted two competing interpretations of vitality in relation to the problem of euthanasia. The major difference between the two interpretations of vitality is that the first consider our inviolability to be unconditional, and the second considers it to be conditional. The first construes vitality within a strict deontological frame and the second rendition takes a teleological orientation. In the first rendition, vitality must be valued for its own sake, and, so long as one has it, we should never kill them, even if it is for the benefit of relieving them from unbearable suffering. We notice that the first view construes vitality within a strict deontological frame. The second interpretation, though vitality is intrinsically valuable, it functions within a particular teleological frame, where the ultimate value of human existence is intertwined with the moral purpose of intensifying or increasing vitality (Chemhuru 2016). Human existence that is detached from this moral purpose of increasing or preserving one's vitality (due to extreme medical conditions), which Tempels (1959: 32) refers to as "the only kind of blessing", may justifiably be euthanized.

Next, I consider the implications of the community view of human dignity for euthanasia.

3.2.2 Community and Euthanasia

In relation to voluntary euthanasia, Metz argues that his view is moderate compared to both utilitarianism and Kant's ethics. In relation to euthanasia, he informs us that he is considering "the very old, or at least those adults who are expected to die soon and are suffering" (Metz 2021: 280). Metz observes that utilitarianism fares well in cases of inevitable and intolerable suffering where the patient will be dying soon. In such a context, Metz observes that utilitarianism would correctly recommend euthanasia. He observes that it struggles in cases involving individual (medical patient) choice or consent. Choice does not register as an important moral consideration in utilitarianism. In a situation where a suffering individual refuses euthanasia, utilitarianism would insist on it for the sake of minimizing suffering for the individual, which view Metz considers to be unpalatable, as it would be wrongly trumping the individual's choice.

Kantian ethics fails, in Metz's view, because it tends to exaggerate the importance of autonomy in moral thought. In a context where a suffering patient elects to be killed for the sake of accelerating relief where death is inevitable, Kantian ethics would correctly permit voluntary euthanasia in respect of the patient's autonomy. Metz observes that a problematic aspect emerges where Kantian ethics would permit

---

directly, or they withhold consent, or they are left in the hands of a proxy, euthanasia is permissible. For cultures that place a premium on consent this might come across as a serious limitation on the part of a vitality-based ethics. In a communitarian culture, where the common good and consensus are centrally defining features for making crucial decisions affecting our lives, this may not be a major concern.

euthanasia in a context of a perfectly healthy individual who, for whatever reason (Metz gives an example of individuals that hold extreme religious beliefs that believe that death is a passage to heaven) autonomously elects to be euthanized. If free and rational choice of a cognitively competent individual is the only important moral consideration, it should follow that a medical practitioner ought to euthanize such an individual, a view Metz considers to be extreme and implausible.

The community view of human dignity, operating on the moral logic of the twin relationships of identity and solidarity, in Metz's view, moderately captures our intuitions regarding euthanasia. Metz observes that a moderate view is one that can accommodate both, on the one hand, individuals consent, and, on the other, what is good for the individual. An account of human dignity that values cooperative relationships (identity), which are transparent and not subordinating, and, equally values securing others' quality of life by avoiding unnecessary harms to them, Metz believes, does the job of securing a promising account of euthanasia. In the case where utilitarianism fails, Metz's account that values cooperative relationships, would not permit euthanasia without their consent since it would amount to the subordination of the subject, which is opposed to the principle of friendliness, where those in such relationship think in terms of a 'we'. Part of being friendly towards someone requires us to take their perspectives and consent into our consideration when we are being friendly towards them. In terms of Kantian ethics, Metz observes that solidarity requires us to truly act for the sake of promoting the welfare of another, in this instance, which requires us "to avoid (a) fate worse than (or equal to) death" (Metz 2021: 282). Failure to do so would amount to "a degrading treatment of his capacity to be helped (and to help others)" (ibid.). The medical practitioner would have failed to be friendly by ensuring the welfare of the religious extremists by refusing to euthanize them.

In light of the above rough comparative analysis of utilitarianism, Kantian ethics and the friendliness view, Metz (2021: 282) comes to this observation: "Choice without good is lacking content; good without choice is misdirected" (ibid.). In this light, he believes that his account of human dignity, in relation to euthanasia, balances out the aspect of choice and that of the good (well-being). It is immoral to conduct euthanasia against someone's will, as it subordinates her (fails to operate on the moral logic of cooperation); and, it is wrong to conduct euthanasia when it is not aimed at securing an individuals' quality of life (fails to properly promote the good of the individual). Roughly, permissible instances of euthanasia would at least accommodate both facets, the facet of identity (sharing a way of life) and solidarity (securing others' quality of life), which balances individuals' choices and their good.[4]

I turn next to personhood and euthanasia.

---

[4]It appears to me that Metz's view might accommodate non-voluntary euthanasia, particularly where the proxy's decision is characteristically done in the spirit of expression friendliness. It will surely oppose involuntary euthanasia because forcefully performing euthanasia against the patient's choice and wishes is blatantly unfriendly.

3.2.3 Personhood and Euthanasia: Ikuenobe's Account

I must admit that it is not immediately clear to me how Ikuenobe's view of human dignity might imply regarding euthanasia. Remember, Ikuenobe accounts for human dignity in terms of the agent developing and positively exercising her capacities for the benefit of the society at large. In his view, human dignity is performance-based insofar as it is something we achieve relative to the quality of our character, which is largely characterized by other-regarding duties. The question we have to answer now is – how can such a view of human dignity account for voluntary euthanasia? If an individual is old, terminally ill and lives under a condition of serious pain and suffering, can this view permit voluntary euthanasia and why?

If an individual has a reached a position where they can no longer develop and exercise their capacities for the benefit of society then it seems, at that point, we can no longer talk of human dignity. As much as we can no longer speak of human dignity, the reader should keep in mind that Ikuenobe still requires us to manifest great respect towards these individuals. In fact, Ikuenobe (2017: 464) believes that we owe such individuals unconditional respect. The normative implications of this unconditional respect owed by moral agents towards individuals in an extreme medical condition are not entirely clear – would it permit voluntary euthanasia? So far as I can tell, we could permit euthanasia by appeal to the virtues intrinsic in the concept of personhood, which can give us a way to make sense of unconditional respect for those who are unable to exercise their capacities, in this instance, imagine the old, who are terminally ill and suffering.

The notion of personhood is associated with relational virtues, which are meant to secure the well-being of everyone in the society. Some of the virtues associated with personhood are those of compassion, kindness, sympathy or even empathy. In fact, Wiredu (1996: 71) informs us that sympathy or empathy, which terms he appears to use interchangeably, is 'the root of all moral virtue'. Part of what might be involved in demonstrating unconditional respect might just entail being compassionate and empathetic towards those unable to exercise their capacities, more so under conditions of extreme suffering. It is not farfetched to suppose that this unconditional respect might be compatible with voluntary euthanasia. I say so because it would be an instantiation of insensitivity or even cruelty towards a frail, suffering and dying individual to simply ignore her pleas for relief through a good death. This insensitivity or cruelty has no place in the kinds of virtues associated with personhood. In this light, it seems that a plausible interpretation of personhood permits us to include voluntary euthanasia in the requirement to unconditionally respect those that are sick and dying.

Notice the nature of this justification for voluntary euthanasia. It is a two-pronged strategy. On the one hand, it points to the fact that it would be unreasonable to place moral responsibilities (related to perfection) on individuals that lack the requisite capacities to do so, either due to disability or being old and frail. It appeals to the principle of "ought implies can" to excuse those that are old frail, sick and dying from the responsibility to pursue human dignity (Ikuenobe 2017: 464). On the other hand, it places the responsibility of unconditional respect on moral agents towards those that cannot so use their capacities. These responsibilities towards the infirm are intrinsically connected with personhood and/or human dignity. It is a function, in part, of what it means to be a person, to have human dignity, which explains the permissibility of voluntary euthanasia. One who has dignity, a moral exemplar, ought to be empathetic towards the frail, suffering and dying for the sake of their own well-being, otherwise, the agent's personhood is at stake. It is by appeal to these virtues associated with personhood that one can justify voluntary euthanasia. The failure to respond positively to cases of voluntary euthanasia is opposed to the kinds of virtues associated with human dignity.

I turn next to consider Molefe's view of human dignity and its implications for euthanasia.

3.2.4 Personhood and Euthanasia: Molefe's Account

In Molefe's interpretation of the personhood-view of human dignity, voluntary euthanasia is permissible. Molefe (2020a) lays out his view on euthanasia in the essay 'Personhood and Euthanasia in African Philosophy'. In unfolding his view on euthanasia, Molefe begins by noting that the idea of a good death is a feature of African thought. The death of a child or a mere adult is considered to be a bad death since these two groups would not have had enough time to pursue and participate in the mission of acquiring virtue (Wiredu 1992: 200). A death, on the other hand, of an elder, a really old individual who has lived well, counts as an instance of a good death. To buttress this view, Molefe approvingly cites Tangwa's (1996: 195) remark that when an "elder who has accomplished his or her mission in life falls sick, s/he would pray that, if her time has come, God take him/her speedily". In this context, death would be seen as a welcome friend rather than a foe to be avoided as much as is possible. At this stage, the elder would be begging for a speedy death, so he can rest from unnecessarily prolonged suffering and shame. The prospect of such a death, which comes as a relief and escape of undue suffering, is surely conceived as a good one.

The point of uncovering the place of a good death in African cultures and thought, on the part of Molefe, I suppose, is to lay a foundation for the permissibility of euthanasia in African thought. The next question then is how he justifies euthanasia by appeal to his view of human dignity, which accounts for it by appeal to our capacity for virtue. Molefe's argument is that the very purpose of human existence is the development of our capacity for virtue, which involves achieving moral perfection or a good character. The possession of the capacity for virtue captures *status dignity* and the actual achievement of virtue captures *achievement dignity* (Michael 2014). The former is inherent, unconditional and is not earned, we have it simply because we possess the capacity for virtue. The latter is extrinsic, conditional and is earned as a consequence of our effort and conduct. The very purpose and meaning of life revolve around being true to what it means to be human, which essentially involves being engaged in the project of achieving virtue (Molefe 2020b).

3.2 Euthanasia

As long as the agent is alive and able, she is required to pursue moral virtue as much as is possible. For one, however, to be able to pursue such an end, surely they ought to be in a reasonably good biological/health condition. An individual that is terminally ill, under immense suffering and pain, and will be dying soon, in Molefe's view, may be euthanized for two major reasons. The first reason involves the fact that the individual has reached a level where she can no longer pursue virtue, which is the essential purpose of human existence. Euthanasia is justified in a context where human existence is meaningless, where 'meaningfulness' is defined by the possibility to exercise one's capacity for virtue. The point is not that human life itself must be meaningful insofar as the agent would have achieved virtue, rather, one should be in a position to live a meaningful life *qua* exercise their highly prized ontological capacity for virtue. In a condition, where such a possibility eludes the agent, voluntary euthanasia is permissible.

The second reason revolves around extrinsic dignity, or the actual achievement of virtue. Molefe (2020a: 120) expresses the second reason in this fashion:

> I propose the view that euthanasia should be permissible in the context where … preservation of a dignified life are threatened or stand to be reversed by extreme medical conditions.

An extrinsic dignity, a state where one's life is characterised by a record of social and moral excellence, should be preserved, rather than left to decay in a context where one is a victim of inescapable suffering and disease, and also a victim of impending death. In such a context, voluntary euthanasia is justified if one's suffering only adds shame to a life that was otherwise exuberant with all kinds of virtues. Embarrassment and shame, associated with being helplessly frail, sick, suffering and dying, ought to be avoided as much as possible. In the context where suffering is pointless (not connected with moral courage or strengthening of other virtues), except for adding shame associated with being helpless, sorrow, misery and unbearable (in this way a disvalue), then voluntary euthanasia is permissible.

In Molefe's view, euthanasia is permissible in contexts where human existence is no longer properly connected to the goal of pursuing or preserving extrinsic dignity. The worst evil that motivates and justifies voluntary euthanasia is when one's life-long achievements would be sullied by the shame of being in a helpless state, only waiting for death to rescue the individual. In this light, Molefe, approvingly quotes Tangwa (1996: 195) "At such ripe old age, the Nso' fear illness and suffering but not death".[5]

In the next section, I turn to animal ethics in light of African theories of human dignity.

---

[5] It strikes me that Molefe's view would permit both non-voluntary and involuntary euthanasia. I say so because the guiding moral consideration is whether the agent can still pursue personhood and/or she can preserve her achievement of dignity. Should she be not in a position to pursue and preserve personhood then it should follow that euthanasia is permissible.

3.3 Animal Ethics

In this section, I turn my attention to the question of animals. Specifically, I want to ascertain the implications of the four theories of human dignity for animals, specifically whether they can assign any place for them in the moral community. To be a part of the moral community requires at least for some entity to have moral status. In this light, we will be considering whether these theories do assign any moral status to animals. Another way to frame our inquiry about animals is in terms of investigating whether the theories of human dignity under consideration are anthropocentric or non-anthropocentric. Anthropocentric theories assign intrinsic value only to human beings (Behrens 2011). On an anthropocentric view, animals do not have value in and of themselves, and, if they matter at all, it is on an indirect or pragmatic basis. Non-anthropocentric views approach or assign value in ways that extend their scope to include non-human components of nature like animals (Horsthemke 2015).

I begin by considering the place of animals in the moral community in light of vitality ethics.

3.3.1 Vitality and Animals

What does an African religious theory of human dignity imply about the status and place of animals in the moral community? Remember, on this view, everything that exists in the cosmos has moral status. The major difference is that, in the physical domain, human beings have the highest quantities of vitality, and, hence, have dignity. Animals, follow directly under the human sphere in the hierarchy, which means they have moral status, which is less than that of human beings. In this light, we can note that animals have lower moral status than human beings, but have greater moral status than inanimate things. From this, we can conclude that animals do have moral status in their own right and for the same reason that human beings do, albeit human beings possess greater moral status than them.

It is worth noting that a vitalist account of value is characterized by two features. On the one hand, a vitalist account is overtly *individualistic* insofar as it accounts for moral status in terms of an internal feature of an individual – the divine energy of vitality. Intrinsic value is a function merely of possessing this feature. If this was all there was to this theory, it would entail that anything and everything that possesses vitality is equal to every other. It is important, however, to note that the vitalist approach is also characterized by moral holism. Holism is a function of the hierarchy that specifies the rank and position, high or low, of all the elements in the cosmos. Though everything has intrinsic value in the world due to possessing vitality, the major difference is a function of its station in the hierarchy. Moreover, and more to the point I seek to make, all entities within the same category in the hierarchy have equal moral status. In other words, on this view, all animals, without exception are equal insofar as they belong to the same rank of being animals.

It is of interest to notice that there is a sense in which the vitalist view can be said to be anthropocentric. It can be said to be anthropocentric insofar as it tends to view human beings as the most important aspect of the cosmos or insofar it takes human beings to be at the center of the cosmos or insofar as it considers human interests' to be more important than those of animals and all other entities in the physical sphere (see Mbiti 1969; Magesa 1997; Bujo 2009). It is equally important, however, to register the fact that it does assign animals some moral status. In this light, we can reasonably conclude that a vitality based approach is anthropocentric, but the kind of anthropocentrism at play here is the weak kind. Here, we draw a distinction between *weak* and *strong* anthropocentrism. Weak anthropocentrism imposes a hierarchy among beings of value, there are those with higher moral status and those with lower moral status. Weak anthropocentrism grants animals and some other components of nature lower moral status, and it assigns a greater moral status to human beings (Norton 1984). Strong anthropocentrism assigns intrinsic value only to human beings, and all other aspects of the environment, have no value at all (Brennan and Lo 2016). If the distinction is true at all, and I believe it to be at least useful, we can conclude that the vitalist account of moral status is characterized by weak anthropocentrism as it assigns non-human components like animals partial moral status.

In this light, we conclude that a vitalist ethic entails that we do have some duties towards animals. We ought not to treat them merely as a resource for human satisfaction. Insofar as animals exist in the universe in a state where they possess vitality and have a place in the hierarchy, it should follow that they have a purpose and matter for their own sakes to some extent (Chemhuru 2016).

Next, I turn to the community view in relation to animals.

3.3.2   Community and Animals

Does the relational or community-based view assign value or moral status to animals? From the outset, Metz (2012: 387) promises to deliver an account that captures the prevalent intuition that "animals and humans both have moral status that is of the same kind but different in degree". In this light, it would seem that Metz considers animals to have moral status and to have it on the same basis as human beings. The difference between animals and human beings, in Metz's view, is that human beings have greater moral status than animals that merely have partial moral status. If Metz is correct, it follows that he can be classified as committed to weak anthropocentrism, as opposed to the strong version of it. Remember, weak anthropocentrism assigns animals some moral status, albeit less than that of human beings.

Here, I wish for us to consider two claims that emerged above. Firstly, I wish for us to consider how Metz accounts for the claim that human beings have greater moral status than animals. Secondly, I wish for us to ascertain the claim that human beings and animals have the same kind of moral status. Remember, for Metz, the major difference between human beings and animals is that the former can both be subjects and objects of the relationships of identity and solidarity (or friendliness).

Those entities that can both be subjects and objects of such relationships have full moral status, or human dignity, which means "typical humans [are] not only are capable of being identified with and being cared for by others (objects), but also can identify with others and care for them (subjects)" (Metz 2021: 238). Those entities that can only be objects of such relationships have partial moral status, which means we can identify with such beings and can also care for them. Metz considers normal adult human beings to be paradigm instances of human dignity. In his view, animals feature mostly as objects of the relationships of identity and solidarity. Below, I consider why Metz considers animals to feature only as objects of identity and solidarity, and thus lacking dignity.

In his recent book, Metz (2021: 240–241) identifies four groupings among animals in relation to moral status, which he understands to come in degrees. He also notes that these groupings are differentiated by the fact that some have greater moral status, others even lower and others none at all. (1) There are those animals that can both be subjects and objects of identity and solidarity, albeit their subjecthood does not guarantee or justify them as having dignity. In this category, he has animals like chimpanzees and gorillas, whose subjectivity, though it manifest the ability to be subjects, is too rudimentary to warrant the ascription of dignity. (2) There are also those animals that are strictly objects of relationships of identity and solidarity. In relation to this group, Metz observes that "We are clearly able to identify with and exhibit solidarity towards giraffes, cows, pigs, goats, sheep, deer, buffalos, dogs, cats, ferrets, and mice". These animals are characterized by some kind of intentionality or goal-directed behavior and sentience, which we can identify with and support in ways that allows them to live their own lives, so far as we can tell. (3) Then there are those animals that, though they can be objects of relationships of identity and solidarity, are much lower in that status "due to their comparative lack of goal-directed behaviour" (ibid.: 241). These animals, Metz gives examples of "molluscs and worm", are objects of friendliness insofar as their welfare can be made better or worse off by our conduct towards them, but it is lower because of their "comparative lack of goal-directed behaviour" or they lack "intentionality" as a characteristic feature of their existence – these animals' operations seem to pivot on instinct (ibid.: 241). (4) Finally, there are those animals that cannot be objects of relationships of identity and solidarity because, Metz informs us, "for all we can tell, they utterly lack both intentionality and a (welfarist) good". He presumes that "mosquitos and bacteria" serve as examples of this category of animals (ibid.).

Now, I consider the second claim that human beings and animals have the same moral status. I consider this claim because it has implications for whether Metz's account is anthropocentric or not. Remember that Metz seeks to secure a unitary basis for the moral status of human beings and animals. It is worth noting, however, that, for Metz, human beings have moral status or even dignity because they can relate to each other in terms of identity and solidarity. Animals, however, have moral status because human beings can relate with them in terms of identity and solidarity. In this way, the basis for moral status pivots on certain aspects of human nature, in a way that they do not in those of animals (Molefe 2017). Notice this comment from Metz (2012: 400, see also 2021: 249):

3.3 Animal Ethics

The theory might appear to be anthropocentric in that it cashes out moral status in terms of certain human capacities. To be able to be an object of a communal relationship, on this view, is analyzed in terms of a capacity to relate to normal human beings in a certain way. And so there is an irreducible appeal to humanity in its conception of moral status.

Notice these claims from the above quotation – *it cashes moral status in terms of certain human capacities* and *there is an irreducible appeal to humanity in its conception of moral status*. These two statements are sufficient to settle the view that Metz's account is anthropocentric insofar as it accounts for all moral value primarily in terms of some features of humanity. In a sense, humanity is a standard of morality in a way that an animal or even an alien may not be, precisely because it is not human. The feature of being human, or, at least capacities definitive of them, specifically, those of identity and solidarity, are essential for defining morality (Molefe 2020a). Given that we are aware that we might draw a distinction between strong and weak forms of anthropocentrism, which form characterizes this view of morality? Metz believes that his view, at most, entails a plausible form of anthropocentrism – probably the weak kind anthropocentrism, as opposed to the strong version of it. He provides two reasons to justify this view.

Firstly, it is able to account for the moral status of animals in their own right. In this light, unlike strong anthropocentrism, it does not consider animals to be a mere resource that we can use without considering their welfare. He argues that since animals can be objects of friendliness, they stand as "proper objects of ethical concern in their own right" (Metz 2012: 400). The second reason observes that the theory is not speciesist, in that it does not base morality merely on the fact of being human *qua* human. In fact, it is capacity-based, the capacity to participate in relationships of identity and solidarity defines moral value, or moral status. Anything that has these capacities, and, can relate with human beings, can have moral status.

Next, I consider the implications of the personhood-based view of human dignity on animals.

3.3.3 Personhood and Animals: Ikuenobe's Account

So far as I am aware, Ikuenobe has never directly applied his work on personhood to the question of the place of animals in the moral community. Furthermore, he does not consider the implication of his account of human dignity to the question of animals. This might preliminarily suggest that his account is anthropocentric. This suggestion should not be surprising given that the idea of personhood, at least as it appears in the writings of Menkiti and Gyekye, is patently anthropocentric in the strong sense. The reader might be familiar with Menkiti's (1984: 177) views on animals:

The foregoing interpretation would incidentally rule out, I believe, some dangerous tendencies currently fashionable in some philosophical circles of ascribing rights to animals. The danger as I see it is that such an extension of moral language to the domain of animals is bound to undermine, sooner or later, the clearness of our conception of what it means to be a person.

Gyekye (1992: 117) seems to also hold a similar view

This conception of a person however, must not be considered as eliminating or writing off children or infants as persons even though they are not (yet) considered as moral agents, as capable of exercising moral sense. The reason is that even though children are not morally capable in actuality, they are morally capable in potentiality. Unlike the colt which will never come to possess a moral sense even if it grew into an adult (horse), children do grow to become *moral* agents on reaching adolescence: at this stage they are capable of exercising their moral sense and thus of making moral Judgments.

Both Menkiti and Gyekye exclude animals from the moral community because they lack the requisite capacity to pursue personhood (Molefe 2015).

A careful reading of Ikuenobe's view strikes me as entailing the same consequence of excluding animals from the moral community. Remember, Ikuenobe grounds human dignity on the notion of personhood. He treats the concept of personhood as a thick concept insofar as it embodies both the descriptive and normative aspects. The descriptive aspect refers to the natural capacities of our human nature and the normative refers to the actual development and exercise of these capacities to be bearers of moral virtue and excellence. In this view, human dignity is constituted by the positive use of our capacities, by way of exhibiting a virtuous character.

If human dignity is a function of the exercise of our capacities, that is, a function of a positive use of our capacities to contribute to communal well-being, then it should follow that animals do not have moral status. The major reason supporting this conclusion is the fact that animals lack the requisite capacity to pursue personhood. If human dignity is a function of pursuing moral perfection then it should follow that any entity that cannot pursue personhood has no moral status at all. It appears to me, given that moral status is connected with the actual achievement of personhood, animals, at best, can be secured on an indirect basis. Here we might appeal to the very status of personhood itself to offer some protections to animals. If, in part, what it means to be a person involves being sympathetic or compassionate to the suffering of others – the 'others' here can be used inclusively to accommodate sentient beings – then it should follow that it is not in keeping with the spirit of virtue to be cruel towards sentient creatures. In this light, even though animals have no intrinsic value, we owe them indirect duties grounded on preserving the quality of our humanity in a fashion similar to the view of protecting animals present in Kant's work.

In this light, we note that Ikuenobe's view is also characterized by some kind of anthropocentrism. It might not be necessarily accurate to classify this view as characterized by strong anthropocentrism. Though this account assigns intrinsic value only to human beings, it offers a personhood-based prudential consideration to be sensitive and responsive to the plight of animals. In this light, unlike Gyekye's and Menkiti's overt strong anthropocentrism, we might associate Ikuenobe's view with *enlightened anthropocentrism* (Brennan and Lo 2016). The defining feature of enlightened anthropocentrism is that it urges us to jettison the search for non-anthropocentric basis to include non-human components in the moral community. It bases our duties to the environment, including animals, on a prudential basis that prioritizes the well-being of human beings and of future generations (Keurlatz 2012).

In terms of personhood, the axiological basis of this prudence is secured by preserving human excellence as a feature of our social, political culture and morality. I leave it to the reader to consider if this strategy to protect animals is sufficient and plausible.

I turn to Molefe's view in relation to animals.

3.3.4 Personhood and Animals: Molefe's Account

The second interpretation of the personhood-based view of human dignity assigns full moral status to human beings and a partial one to animals. In this sense, it might be construed as a version of a weak kind of anthropocentrism. Remember, Molefe's view is a capacity-based view of human dignity, where the capacity for virtue secures human dignity. If this information was all we have, it would follow that only human beings have human dignity since they possess the requisite capacity to pursue virtue (as we have seen in Menkiti and Gyekye above) and animals do not possess it. How then does Molefe associate his view with weak anthropocentrism? Molefe follows the strategy employed by Metz, where he distinguishes between those entities that can both be subjects and objects of virtue (i.e. those entities that can actually pursue the project of moral excellence and can be positively benefitted by virtuous disposition or conduct towards them) from those entities than can only be objects of virtue (i.e., those that can be positively benefitted by virtue). Molefe (2020a: 88) endorses this interpretation in this fashion:

> The reader will notice that, here, I am employing the strategy employed by Metz, where I distinguish between entities that can be subjects and objects of moral perfection (full moral status) and those that can largely be objects of moral perfection (partial moral status). If this interpretation of moral status in the light of those entities that can be subjects and those that can be objects is correct, it follows that it assigns animals some moral status.

One of the central considerations that qualifies animals for being objects of virtue is that many of them are sentient. Molefe (2020a, b), in some places, defines virtue in terms of sympathy, and this entails that subjects of virtue must be open, sensitive and responsive to other sentient beings like animals. The idea of subjects of virtue being 'open' suggests that they should not unnecessarily limit or narrow the bowels of their compassion only to human beings. Or, this idea could be expressed to be a call to move away from unjustified or arbitrary fixation only on the interests of human beings. Animals, since they can suffer and their interests frustrated in many ways, should enter as inputs in the moral calculus of moral agents when they contemplate how to act in the world and towards them. The perfectionism associated with personhood entails that we have some duties, though weaker than those we have towards human beings, towards animals (since the latter are only objects of virtue). It is also in the interest of the agent's project of moral perfection to develop her sensibilities and sensitivities towards animals, which is consistent with the standards of moral excellence.

In the next section, I turn to the question of disability in light of the salient theories of human dignity.

3.4 Disability Ethics

This section explores the question of disability in light of African theories of human dignity. Specifically, it aims to consider the place of people living with disabilities, particularly those who are seriously mentally disabled, in the moral community in light of African thought. By 'disabled individuals', in this chapter, I have in mind individuals with cognitive disabilities. I am aware that we can distinguish between *mild*, *moderate* and *severe* cognitive disabilities (Wasserman et al. 2017). My focus will be on what has variously been described in the literature in moral philosophy as "severe", "significant" or, "radical" cognitive or mental disabilities (Nussbaum 2002: 134; Kittay 2005: 102 & 109; 2011: 51; Singer 2009: 568; McMahan 2009: 240). I adopt the definition of severe cases of mental disability proffered by Peter Singer, which identifies such cases in terms of at least five elements, namely: (1) have a low IQ of 25 and below; (2) require much supervision for day-to-day life activities; (3) they generally lack speech, writing and reading abilities; (4) general lack of ability to do useful and productive work (though, in some cases, with training this might change) and (5) generally lack social skills.

This definition of profoundly mentally injured individuals finds corroboration in the writings of a leading feminist, Eva Feder Kittay. What is interesting about Kittay's definition is that it offers a concrete definition of disability that she draws from the lived experience of her daughter, Sesha, who is significantly mentally impaired. Kittay (2005: 99–100, emphasis mine) makes this illuminating comment that depicts *a* real-life picture of an individual that is seriously impaired:

> There are people with disabilities such as my daughter who, no matter what resources are made available and no matter what prejudices are banished, will be (seemingly, at least) *incapable of fashioning their lives as they see fit*; *who do not evidently exhibit the capacities to engage in moral practical reasoning* ...; and *who cannot function reciprocally in a scheme of social co-operation* ... And yet they can experience human joy, human relationships, benefit from habilitation, from artistic experiences and so forth. They can give and receive love — even if it cannot always be manifested in usual ways. Still people such as *Sesha can never be independent and productive and it is not at all clear that they can ever be moral agents.*

I look into the question of disability in general largely because it is a neglected theme in the literature in African philosophy. Moreover, I delimit my scope to the case of individuals that are profoundly mentally impaired for reasons already specified in the literature in moral philosophy:

> Our reason for limiting ourselves to cognitive impairment is dialectical: there is currently no debate about the moral status of individuals with non-cognitive disabilities. We know of no serious philosopher who argues that people who cannot see, hear, or use their legs, or who experience frequent depression or hallucinations, have lower moral status than people without such disabilities (Wasserman et al. 2017).

This quotation specifies a reason why moral philosophers have tended to focus on cases of severe mental impairment. The first reason is the fact that in the literature in moral philosophy, no one disputes the moral status or even dignity of other kinds of disability (being blind, deaf, etc.). These cases have not dominated the literature precisely because they do not raise doubts or questions about the moral status of those that have such disabilities. The case of individuals with serious mental disabilities is of philosophical importance because it is intrinsically connected with the question of their moral status. In the context of the Western tradition of philosophy, the case of profound mental impairments is crucial because of the prime placed on rationality, autonomy, self-determination in ethical discourse (Kittay 2011). The essence of the debate is – do we exclude mentally disabled individuals from the moral community or do we look beyond the influential rationality-based based ethics in the "the construction of an ethics of inclusion" (Kittay 2011: 51).

Since the question of the place and status of the severely mentally disabled individuals is largely under-explored in the tradition of African philosophy, it (African philosophy) might offer us a novel perspective on this theme given that it does not tend to place a prime on rationality or autonomy. Hence, in what follows, I will consider the case of individuals that are severely mentally impaired in light of vitality, community and personhood.

I begin with the case of vitality and disability.

3.4.1 Vitality and Disability

Remember that on vitality ethics, moral status is a function of merely possessing vitality or life force. Those entities with higher degrees of vitality in the physical sphere, specifically, human beings, have dignity. Above, I have already noted that this view of moral status and/or human dignity is at once, individualistic, and it equally has a feature of holism. Its individualism is a function of the mere possession of vitality, which assigns all entities moral status. Its holism is a function of the position occupied by different species in the hierarchy characteristic of the African conception of reality. In other words, all entities within each segment of the hierarchy have equal moral status or human dignity. It is important to get a clear sense of the interaction of the individualism and holism characteristic of the vitality ethics.

The mere possession of vitality, which is a feature or attribute of the individual, accommodates the entity within the moral community, or into the moral sphere, where it becomes a rightful object of ethical concern. The moral holism aspect functions primarily to stratify the moral community, and to properly position each entity where it belongs, and thus clarify the extent of our moral duties towards it. Without the individual deposit of vitality into entities there would be no talk of moral status. Without the hierarchy that stratifies the moral community into differentially ranked sub-communities, there would not be clarity regarding the nature and scope of our moral duties inter-and-intra-species. In light of this clarification, we can then make a determination about the place of the severely mentally impaired individuals in light of vitality ethics.

On this view, severely mentally disabled individuals, in light of the individual deposit of the divine energy of vitality, have moral status. In this light, they are proper objects of ethical concern, owed duties for their own sakes. Moreover, given that they belong to the higher strata of the sub-community of the human community, which has human dignity, we observe that they also have human dignity. This is the case because of the moral holism characteristic of vitality ethics. Moral holism assigns moral status, ultimately, on the basis of merely belonging to the group without regard to the attributes of individuals within a group. Dion (1987: 223) affirms this view in this fashion: "... although the individual member has fewer abilities than its own species, it has the same intrinsic value as that of its own species". The point should be clear by now, though the severely mentally injured persons have fewer abilities than an average adult human being (which fact is beside the point when it comes to assigning moral status), they have full moral status. The human dignity of severely mentally impaired individuals remains intact merely because she belongs to the human strata that enjoy this full moral status.

I hope it is clear that the African view of vitality assigns moral status to everything that possesses vitality – this is a function of moral individualism. Further, we noted that all human beings have higher moral status or even dignity because they possess higher quantities of vitality. We explained human beings' dignity by appeal to moral holism, which is a function of the high rank they occupy in the hierarchy. We can conclude, in light of the vitality based view of human dignity that severely mentally disabled individuals have full moral status because they belong to the human strata in the hierarchy, which possesses higher quantities of vitality.

In the next section, I turn to the implications of the community view of human dignity for individuals that are mentally disabled.

3.4.2   Community and Disability

It is worth noting that Metz in his exposition and defense of the community view of human dignity does consider the case of mentally disabled individuals. To get a sense of Metz's approach and view on the question of seriously mentally disabled individuals, it is important to compare it to Peter Singer's approach. Singer (2009) in his essay 'Speciesism and Moral Status' compares severely mentally disabled individuals and animals. He does this comparison primarily to question two central moral intuitions in moral philosophy: (1) all human beings have equal moral status and (2) all human beings have a moral status superior to that of animals. He ultimately defends what he calls "a graduated view that applies to animals as well as to humans" (2009: 567). I understand this mean, there are cases where we will have animals with greater moral status than some human beings, *vice versa*. My interest, in his essay, is the strategy he employs to pursue his argument.

The strategy Singer employs involves comparing human individuals – those that are severely mentally disabled – with (normal adult) animals. Singer then proceeds to provide evidence to the effect that we have animals (gorillas, chimpanzees, parrots

3.4 Disability Ethics

and dogs) that have superior cognitive abilities than some human beings (particularly those that are severely mentally disabled). He argues that the reasons often adduced to support the two central intuitions – the moral equality of all human beings and their superior moral status to all animals – ultimately fail to secure the desired conclusion.

I suspect Metz (2012: 387) being aware of Singer's approach and its conclusions, sets himself the goal to secure the prevalent intuition that "even a severely mentally incapacitated human being has a greater moral status than an animal ..." I caution the reader that I cut out an important part of the quotation, which I believe will show the difference between Metz's approach to that of Singer. Metz seeks to secure the intuition that (I now add the part I had omitted) "even a severely mentally incapacitated human being has a greater moral status than an animal *with identical internal properties*" (ibid., emphasis mine). Singer, on his part, focuses on the fact that there are many animals with better or superior abilities than human beings particularly if you take cognitive abilities as the basis for moral status. Whereas, Metz considers the cases of severely mentally disabled individuals that have comparably equal internal properties with animals, be they cognitive or otherwise. In this light, we duly note that Metz only considers cases of serious mental disability where human beings possess identical internal properties with animals. He does not, unlike Singer, consider the case where animals possess superior internal properties than human beings.

Now that we have a sense of how Metz contextualizes his approach, we can proceed to consider two related considerations – (1) how does Metz justify the view that severely mentally injured individuals have moral status? and (2) how does Metz justify the view that their moral status is greater than that of animals with identical internal properties. Metz assigns partial moral status to severely mentally disabled individuals on the basis that they can be objects of communal relations. In other words, though severely mentally disabled individuals may not initiate relationships of identity and solidarity, they can benefit (in terms of welfare) from such relationships, i.e. such relationships directed towards them can make their lives better or worse off, in a way that they cannot benefit or even harm a stone. Though many of the severely mentally individuals may lack goal-directed behaviour (or, what we may call intentionality), they still remain sentient, and, on that ground, can be harmed or made better off. Hence, this comment by Metz (2012: 397)

> However, the African theory does appear to entail that severely mentally incapacitated human beings ... lack a dignity comparable to ours, for they are incapable of being subjects of a communal relationship.

The above explains the part involving how we might justify the claim that severely mentally incapacitated individuals have moral status, though they lack dignity since they cannot be subjects of identity and solidarity. The second consideration involves how Metz justifies the claim that severely mentally disabled individuals have greater moral status than animals with identical internal properties. Metz (2012: 397) argues in this fashion:

> Compared with animals, normal human beings are more able to include "deformed" humans such as psychopaths, as well as the mentally incapacitated, in a "we", cooperate with them, act in ways likely to improve their quality of life, exhibit sympathetic emotions with them, and act for their sake. We do much more for the psychopathic and the mentally incapacitated than we do animals, which is evidence of a greater ability to make them an object of a friendly relationship.

The essence of the argument seems to be that it is easier for us to enter into relationships of identity and solidarity with severely mentally disabled human beings than it is for us to enter into such relationships with animals. Or, put another way, severely mentally disabled individuals possess a greater capacity to be objects of communal relations than animals. The evidence to buttress the claim that severely disabled individuals have a greater capacity to be objects of communal relations, according to Metz, is that we tend do much more for them than we do for animals. It might be true that we have a history of doing more for mentally disabled human beings than we do for animals. It remains unclear, however, how this empirical fact serves as a principled explanation for the claim that the former have a greater capacity to be objects of identity and solidarity than the latter.

It occurs to me that we need an explanation that cannot easily be eclipsed by considerations of human prejudice, where they favour their kind over animals (speciesism). If these two have identical internal properties (whatever the significance of this qualifier might be), what are the crucial consideration(s) about the severely mentally disabled human beings that sets them apart and above animals, which will explain why we tend do more for them? To get the force of this question consider the fact that racists tend to do more for those of their race. From the behaviour of racists, it does not follow that members of a particular racial group (A) have greater capacity to be objects of identity and solidarity than those who do not belong to their race (B). It is possible that some other consideration is doing the job of explaining the tendency of A doing more for persons who are A – arbitrary race-based discriminations. The kind of evidence invoked by Metz is not clear cut enough to rule out crude speciestic consideration as the basis for our tendency to do more for other human beings?

Anyways, the point is not to unfold a critical treatment of Metz's view but rather to unfold its implications for the severely mentally handicapped human beings. We note that Metz's view accounts for the moral status of severely mentally disabled individuals by appeal to the claim that these can be objects of the relationships of identity and solidarity. Those that are mentally disabled have greater moral status than animals at least those animals with comparatively similar internal properties because the former have a greater capacity to be objects of identity and solidarity than do animals.

In the next section, I consider Ikuenobe's personhood-based view of human dignity in relation to the mentally disabled.

3.4 Disability Ethics

3.4.3 Personhood and Disability: Ikuenobe's Account

The reader will remember that Ikuenobe's view of human dignity grounds it in the thick concept of personhood. On the one hand, the concept of personhood has metaphysical capacities and, on the other, it has the normative dimension, which involves the development of a "virtuous character" and the requirement for the agent to "use one's capacity to promote loving and caring communal living" (Ikuenobe 2017: 462 & 464). Essential to this view of human dignity is that it construes it as the kind of a value or status we achieve relative to the perfection of our moral characters and the exercise of our duties to promote the greater good. One crucial implication of Ikuenobe's view is that it implies that the requisite capacities that need to be developed and used, in and of themselves, raw and undeveloped, have no intrinsic value. In fact, he is very clear that such metaphysical capacities only have instrumental value.

In this light, we might then pose a question about the moral standing of severely mentally disabled individuals. Since those individuals with such serious disabilities cannot and will never develop and use their capacities to achieve virtue and promote communal well-being, do they have moral status or human dignity? Upon first approximation, it might be tempting to simply assume that those with severe mental disabilities have no moral status or human dignity since they obviously cannot develop and use their capacities to achieve virtue, which essentially involves the promotion of the common good. This temptation might be justified by the fact that Ikuenobe actually holds the view that ontological capacities only amount to, or produce, dignity when used positively for the benefit of the community. It is obvious that the severely mentally disabled individuals cannot exercise their capacities.

I suggest that we need to overcome this temptation by considering two interesting claims in Ikuenobe's adumbrations of his view of human dignity. I suspect that Ikuenobe makes these claims because he is aware of the challenge posed by the severely mentally disabled in light of his account of human dignity. The first claim emerges when Ikuenobe (2017: 459) remarks that the mere possession of the "[c]apacity may imply moral respect in situations where one is not able to use one's capacity". Though, all things being equal, Ikuenobe considers capacities to have no intrinsic value, at most, they only have instrumental value. In this instance, however, where one considers the severely mentally disabled, among others, who are not able to develop and use their capacities, we are informed that capacities may imply moral respect.

It is not clear what kind of respect is anticipated here. It is not off the mark to suppose that it is a weak kind of respect than the one we usually associate with human dignity at least in his account. I say so because of the language employed by Ikuenobe to suggest this is a weak kind of respect. Notice that Ikuenobe states that capacity *may imply* respect, and not, *must imply* respect. The force of 'may' is modal and the force of 'must' is imperative. In other words, *may* merely suggest that there may be circumstances where having a capacity might entail respect. It is not entirely unclear if the respect imagined here is directly connected to the capacity itself of the one that cannot use it or it arises in light of indirect considerations, where the focus is in the capacities of those agents in the community who are able to use them positively in relation to those that can not use them. Those that can use their capacities to develop and preserve the quality of their humanity, ought to respect those that have such capacities but cannot use them like the severely mentally disabled. Surely, this kind of indirect defense of the severely mentally disabled will not satisfy many of us that hold the intuition that the severely mentally disabled do have intrinsic value, be it partial or full.

Ikuenobe's (2017: 464) second claim regarding the status of the severely mentally disabled is more daring:

> My view implies that we have unconditional responsibility to respect, love and care for those (children, those with mental or physical disability) who lack the ability to use their capacity to earn respect . . . The idea of respecting unconditionally those who are not capable of acting to earn respect is supported by the moral principle of 'ought implies can', which indicates that you cannot hold people responsible for what is impossible for them. Dignity involves respect for one's God-given capacity for communal living, but for those who are able to use such capacity freely, there is an added element of accountability, which is that respect depends on meeting one's responsibility to use one's capacity to promote loving and caring communal living.

In this instance, Ikuenobe positively argues that his view entails that we have unconditional responsibility to respect, love and care for those with mental disabilities. He appeals to the principle of 'ought implies can' to secure the view that we owe unconditional respect towards the mentally disabled. The essence of this principle is that we cannot hold people responsible for what they cannot do, which principle I believe is correct. It will be quite unreasonable of us to expect severely mentally disabled individuals to pursue personhood, or human dignity, since they lack the essential capacities necessary for such a task in the first place.

In light of the above, we notice that Ikuenobe appears to be proposing two bases for assigning respect. Unconditional respect is reserved for individuals for merely possessing their God-given capacity even if they cannot use them (for reasons beyond their control like being seriously mentally disabled). On the other hand, conditional respect is reserved for individuals that can develop and use their capacities. Those individuals that go on to develop and use their capacities positively have dignity, and we owe them conditional respect.

If the above distinction is true, it follows that we are stuck with two fundamental claims on the moral nature of capacities. The first claim regards capacities to only have instrumental value. In this light, respect is earned and conditional upon the development and positive use of these capacities, which is tantamount to human dignity. The second claim affirms that capacities, in and of themselves, in contexts where one cannot use them, deserve unconditional respect. The unconditional respect pronounced here is not related to performance, and, therefore, it is not earned. If the above analysis is true, it seems to imply that for Ikuenobe human dignity is fundamentally conditional upon positive moral conduct. And, there is another group of individuals, whom we owe unconditional respect because they lack the ability to exercise their capacities. There are two difficulties associated with Ikuenobe's view, which I will briefly highlight.

On the one hand, it is not clear what unconditional respect implies, with regards to the moral status of severely mentally disabled individuals. If unconditional respect is based on the mere possession of a capacity (though seriously marred) then it should follow that the capacity, in and of itself, has intrinsic value – this interpretation is not consistent with Ikuenobe's overall moral philosophy. Or, if unconditional respect implies indirect duties for moral agents, where the agents act out of concern of preserving their own humanity and promoting communal well-being (which involves the good of the severely mentally disabled). I suspect indirect duties will not satisfy many of us that require a stronger basis to protect the interests and rights of the severely mentally disabled. The second difficulty is related to the kind of evidence adduced to buttress the unconditional respect for the severely mentally disabled members of the community. The principle of 'ought implies can' at most settles the fact that we cannot hold the severely mentally disabled individuals responsible for what they cannot do. It does not follow, I insist, that because the severely mentally disabled are unable to pursue personhood that we should grant them unconditional respect (Molefe 2019). It appears to me, we need another principle or some other explanation to secure the basis for unconditional respect. As things stand, it seems, the most useful strategy will involve, appealing to an indirect consideration of protecting our personhood. Even if we take the indirect route to secure the standing of severely mentally disabled individuals, such a solution, at best, secure a less than satisfactory ground than a whole package of rights or duties associated with human dignity (particularly as articulated in the Universal Declaration of Human Rights).

In the final analysis, we observe that Ikuenobe is committed to the view that we do have unconditional duties of respect for the severely mentally disabled. His account of human dignity operates on the moral logic of conditional respect, the condition being the requirement to develop and positively use one's capacities. It remains unclear whether beings that are owed unconditional respect (like the severely mentally disabled) also have moral status or human dignity given the conditional nature of this status. At best, I suggest, we might interpret Ikuenobe to be securing unconditional respect on the duties intrinsic in the requirement for the agent to morally perfect herself, which might involve loving and caring for vulnerable members of the group like the severely mentally disabled for our own sakes.

I turn now to Molefe's personhood-based view of human dignity and its implications for the severely mentally disabled.

3.4.4   Personhood and Disability: Molefe's Account

The reader will remember that Molefe advocates a capacity-based view of moral status or human dignity. He grounds human dignity on the capacity for virtue. Those entities that can both be subjects and objects of virtue have full moral status (or human dignity), and, therefore, deserve utmost moral respect. Those entities that can only be objects of virtue have partial moral status. In Molefe's view, severely mentally disabled individuals present only as objects of virtue. They present only as objects of virtue because they cannot pursue personhood, but they can benefit from other-regarding virtues associated with personhood. In other words, they can be made better off by the kindness, compassion, generosity, and so on, typical of virtuous persons.

If this line of reasoning is correct, it should follow that, according to Molefe, severely mentally disabled individuals and animals enter the moral community on the ticket of their status as objects of virtue. Does this mean that Molefe ranks equally the severely mentally disabled individuals and animals? In his own writings, Molefe (2020c: 99) is not entirely clear what his position is with regards to this question:

> The point of this section is to outline a preliminary, and by all means, rough response to questions regarding animals and the mentally disabled. It suffices to appreciate that animals and mentally disabled individuals are secured their moral standing on the basis, at minimum, that they can be objects of sympathy. Even those animals that can be subjects of sympathy can only be so in a limited way since they cannot pursue and develop personhood in the fullest sense of the term.

In this light, it seems Molefe is comfortable only to specify the minimum standard that grants severely mentally disabled individuals partial moral status. He does not, however, venture into the comparisons that we saw above in relation to Singer's and Metz's adumbrations. We might however theoretically speculate about how Molefe might deal with this comparison. One might do well to remember that Molefe's view is characterised by weak anthropocentrism. We noted that the defining feature of weak anthropocentrism is that it assigns a greater moral status to human beings than animals. In this light, it seems that the kind of prioritizing the human, associated with weak anthropocentrism might justify why, though, severely mentally impaired individuals and animals, are objects of moral status, the latter has greater moral status.

This general ranking of all human beings higher than animals might be justified by the fact that the perfectionism associated with African personhood is the "*human nature perfectionism*" as opposed to the "objective goods perfectionism" (Wall 2012). With the former, the human good is accounted essentially with the development of human nature. Molefe (2019: 10) explains his approach to personhood in this fashion – "I advocate the humanistic and perfectionist . . . view of personhood as a moral theory". At this stage, Molefe might insist on the basis of the humanistic orientation of his moral theory that severely mentally disabled individuals have greater moral status than animals.

3.5 Conclusion

This chapter explored select themes in applied ethics in light of African theories of human dignity. It specifically focused on the themes of euthanasia, animal ethics and the moral standing of the severely mentally disabled. The vitality based view of human dignity has the following implications for the three applied ethics cases: it permits voluntary euthanasia; given that it embodies weak anthropocentrism, it assigns partial moral status to animals and it grants full moral status to severely mentally disabled individuals. The community-based view entails the following regarding the three cases: it permits voluntary euthanasia; it promises to embody the weak version of anthropocentrism, which assigns partial moral status to animals; and it also assigns partial moral status to severely mentally disabled individuals. The first personhood-based view of human dignity has the following implications for the three applied ethics cases: it might permit voluntary euthanasia; it does not assign animals any moral status and it demands unconditional respect for the severely disabled (but on a different ground than that of human dignity). The second view of personhood entails the following conclusions regarding the three cases: it permits voluntary euthanasia, it grants partial moral status to animals and it assigns partial moral status to severely mentally disabled individuals.

In future research, it remains urgent that we take on a more creative and critical project in relation to the concept of human dignity in African philosophy. The anticipated project will make its primary pursuit the search for a plausible theory of human dignity and its consequences for applied ethics, among others. This search will be important as it might also involve comparison with other competing traditions of philosophy like the Chinese philosophy. For now, it suffices for the reader to have a philosophical picture of extant and under-explored theories of human dignity.

References

Beauchamp T, Davidson A (1978) The definition of euthanasia. J Med Philos 4:294–312
Behrens K (2011) African philosophy, thought and practice and their contribution to environmental ethics. University of Johannesburg, Johannesburg
Brennan A, Lo Y (2016) Environmental ethics. In: Zalta EN (ed) The Stanford encyclopedia of philosophy. https://plato.stanford.edu/archives/sum2021/entries/ethics-environmental/
Brock D (1993) Voluntary active euthanasia. Hastings Cent Rep 22:10–22
Bujo B (2009) Ecology and ethical responsibility from an African perspective. In: Murove F (ed) African ethics: an anthology of comparative and applied ethics. University of Kwa-Zulu Natal Press, Pietermaritzburg, pp 391–411
Chemhuru M (2016) The import of African ontology for environmental ethics. University of Johannesburg, Johannesburg
Dion M (1987) The moral status of non-human beings and their ecosystems. Ethics Place Environ 3: 221–229
Gyekye K (1992) Person and community in African thought. In: Wiredu K, Gyekye K (eds) Person and community: Ghanaian philosophical studies, 1. Council for Research in Values and Philosophy, Washington, DC, pp 101–124
Horsthemke K (2015) Animals and African ethics. Palgrave Macmillan, New York
Ikuenobe P (2017) The communal basis for moral dignity: an African perspective. Philos Pap 45: 437–469
Iroegbu P (2005) Do all persons have a right to life? In: Iroegbu P, Echekwube A (eds) Kpim of morality ethics: general, special and professional. Heinemann Educational Books, Ibadan, pp 78–83
Keurlatz J (2012) The emergence of enlightened anthropocentrism in ecological restoration. Nat Cult 7:48–71

Kittay E (2005) Equality, dignity and disability. In: Waldron A, Lyons F (eds) Perspectives on equality: the second Seamus Heaney lectures. Liffey, Dublin, pp 95–122

Kittay E (2011) The ethics of care, dependence and disability. Ratio Juris 24:49–58

Magesa L (1997) African religion: the moral traditions of abundant life. Orbis Books, New York

Mbiti J (1969) African religions and philosophy. Doubleday and Company, New York

McMahan J (2009) Radical cognitive limitation. In: Brownlee K, Cureton A (eds) Disability and disadvantage. Oxford University Press, New York, pp 240–259

Menkiti I (1984) Person and community in African traditional thought. In: Wright RA (ed) African philosophy: an introduction. University Press of America, Lanham, pp 171–181

Metz T (2012) An African theory of moral status: a relational alternative to individualism and holism. Ethical Theory Moral Pract: Int Forum 14:387–402

Metz T (2021) A relational moral theory: African ethics in and beyond the continent. Oxford University Press, Oxford

Michael L (2014) Defining dignity and its place in human rights. New Bioeth 20:12–34

Molefe M (2015) A rejection of humanism in the African moral tradition. Theoria 143:59–77

Molefe M (2017) A critique of Thad Metz's African theory of moral status. S Afr J Philos 36:195–205

Molefe M (2019) An African philosophy of personhood, morality and politics. Palgrave Macmillan, New York

Molefe M (2020a) An African ethics of personhood and bioethics: a reflection on abortion and euthanasia. Palgrave Macmillan, New York

Molefe M (2020b) Personhood and a meaningful life in African philosophy. S Afr J Philos 39:194–207

Molefe M (2020c) African personhood and applied ethics. NISC (PTY).LTD, Grahamstown

Ncayiyana D (2012) Euthanasia – no dignity in death in the absence of an ethos of respect for human life. S Afr Med J 102:334–335

Norton B (1984) Environmental ethics and weak anthropocentrism. Environ Ethics 6:131–148

Nussbaum M (2002) Capabilities and disabilities: justice for mentally disabled citizens. Philos Top 30:133–165

Schroeder D, Bani-Sadr A (2017) Dignity in the 21st century Middle East and West. SpringerOpen, New York

Shutte A (2001) Ubuntu: an ethic for a new South Africa. Cluster Publications, Pietermaritzburg

Singer P (2009) Speciesism and moral status. Metaphilosophy 40(3-4):567–581

Tangwa G (1996) Bioethics: an African perspective. Bioethics 10:183–200

Tempels P (1959) Bantu philosophy (C. King, Trans.). Présence Africaine, Paris

Wall S (2012) Perfectionism in moral and political philosophy. In: Zalta E (ed) The Stanford encyclopedia of philosophy. http://plato.stanford.edu/archives/win2012/entries/perfectionism-moral/

Wasserman, D, Asch A, Blustein J, Putnam D (2017) Cognitive disability and moral status. In: Zalta EN (ed) The Stanford encyclopedia of philosophy. https://plato.stanford.edu/archives/fall2017/entries/cognitive-disability/

Wiredu K (1992) Moral foundations of an African culture. In: Wiredu K, Gyekye K (eds) Person and community: Ghanaian philosophical studies, 1. The Council for Research in Values and Philosophy, Washington, DC, pp 192–206

Wiredu K (1996) Cultural universals and particulars: an African perspective. Indiana University Press, Indianapolis

Wreen M (1988) The definition of euthanasia. Philos Phenomenol Res 48:637–653

Young R (2007) Medically assisted death. Cambridge University Press, Cambridge

Index

A
Abortion, 3, 34, 40, 49, 50
Absolute death, 23, 50
Achievement, 12, 19, 33, 35, 38–40, 43, 54, 55, 60
Achievement dignity, 6, 7, 42, 43, 54
Africa, viii, 2, 3, 27
African ethics, 21, 26, 27, 32
African metaphysics, 20–22, 24
African perspectives, 1, 4, 18, 37
African philosophy, 1–13, 17–44, 47, 54, 62, 63, 71
Agent centred, 34, 35, 37, 40–42
Ancestors, 21, 22, 25
Animal ethics, 2, 12, 47–71
Animals, 8, 9, 12, 21, 22, 31, 32, 40, 43, 56–61, 64–66, 70, 71
Anthropocentric (weak, enlightened, strong anthropocentrism), 57, 59–61, 70
Applied ethics, 2–4, 12–13, 40, 47, 48, 70, 71
Attributed dignity, 9
Autonomy, vii, 1, 5, 6, 17, 18, 37, 39, 51, 63
Axiology, 1, 61

B
Basic capabilities, 6, 18
Behrens, K., 11, 12, 34, 36, 40, 56
Bioethics, 2, 3, 12, 40
Bujo, B., 23, 25, 50, 57

C
Capacity-based, 6, 19, 41, 59, 61, 69
Capacity for communal relations, 11
Capacity for identity and solidarity, 31, 43, 59, 66
Capacity for virtue, 12, 42, 43, 54, 55, 61, 69
Capital punishment, 3
Catholic, 49
Cloning, 3
Cognitive disabilities, 62
Common goals, 28, 29
Communitarians, 27, 34, 51
Communities, viii, 2, 4, 10, 11, 19–22, 26–35, 37, 38, 43, 51–52, 57–59, 63–69
Conceptual models, 6
Conditional respect, 68, 69
Contested nature, 4–6, 10
Contingent obstacles, 32
Cooperation, 52

D
Decolonial, 3
Decolonizing, vii, 3, 20
Degradation, 8
Dehumanization, 8
Deontological frame, 51
Dependency, 18
Different senses, 4, 6–9
Disability ethics, 2, 12, 13, 43, 47, 48, 62–70
Divine Command Theory, 23

E
Egalitarianism, 3, 41
Empathy, 29, 49, 53
Empowerment, 9, 10
Equality, 10, 40, 65

© The Author(s), under exclusive license to Springer Nature Switzerland AG 2022
M. Molefe, *Human Dignity in African Philosophy*, SpringerBriefs in Philosophy,
https://doi.org/10.1007/978-3-030-93217-6

Essentially contested, 5
Ethical naturalism, 23, 26
Ethical supernaturalism, 10, 23
Ethics, 9–11, 20, 22, 23, 26, 36, 37, 40, 48–50, 56, 57, 63, 64
Euthanasia (involuntary, voluntary), 55
Extreme medical conditions, 12, 48, 50, 51, 53, 55
Extrinsic dignity, 55

F
Friendliness, 8, 28, 29, 32, 52, 57–59
Future generations, 61

G
Global south, 2
Good death, 48, 53, 54
Gyekye, K., 3, 4, 6, 11, 33–35, 37, 40, 42, 59–61

H
Harmonious relationships, 19, 27–32, 38, 39, 43
Hierarchy, 22, 24, 25, 43, 56, 57, 63, 64
High status, 7–9
Holism, 31, 56, 63
Human, vii, 1, 3–12, 17–19, 21, 22, 24–26, 28–33, 35, 36, 39, 40, 42, 43, 48–51, 54–66, 70
Human dignity, vii, viii, 1–13, 17–43, 47–71
Human enhancement, 3
Human nature, 1, 7, 10, 17–20, 31–33, 36, 40, 42, 58, 60, 70
Human rights, vii, 1, 3, 37, 42
Humiliation, 8

I
Identity, 28–32, 39, 43, 52, 57–59, 65, 66
Ikuenobe, P., 3, 4, 6, 11, 12, 32, 34, 37–40, 43, 48, 53–54, 59–61, 66–69
Image of god, vii, 6, 18, 25, 49
Individualism, 31, 63, 64
Individualistic, 31, 33, 56, 63
Inflorescent dignity, 7, 9
Inherent dignity, 7
Intentionality, 58, 65
Internal features, 56
Intrinsic dignity, 6–9, 43
Intrinsic worth, 1, 18

Inviolability, 9, 49–51

J
Justice, 3, 38, 41

K
Kantian ethics, 51, 52
Kant's ethics, 51

L
Legal, vii, 1, 3, 9, 50

M
Menkiti, I., 11, 21, 33–37, 40–42, 59–61
Meta-ethical, 18, 22, 23
Metaphysical holism, 20, 21
Metaphysical monism, 20, 21
Metz, T., 3, 10, 11, 25–33, 36, 43, 48, 51, 52, 57–59, 61, 64–66, 70
Modal relationalism, 31
Molefe, M., 3, 4, 6, 10–12, 20, 22, 24, 30, 32, 34, 36, 39–43, 48, 54–55, 58–61, 69–70
Moral community, 12, 13, 39, 40, 47, 56, 59, 60, 62, 63, 70
Moral constraint, 9
Moral death, 50
Moral excellence, 7, 9, 12, 19, 35, 40, 42, 43, 55, 61
Moral holism, 56, 63, 64
Moral perfectionism, 36
Moral purpose, 50, 51
Moral status, 9, 24, 26, 31, 32, 34, 40, 47, 49, 56–67, 69–71

N
Negative approach, 5, 6, 8
Non-anthropocentric, 12, 56, 60
Normative concept of Personhood, 19, 34, 36, 40
Nussbaum, M., 2, 6, 13, 18, 62

O
Ontological personhood, 10, 33, 34, 37, 39, 43, 67
Ought implies can, 53, 68, 69

Index

P

Partiality, 30
Partial moral status, 12, 32, 57, 58, 61, 65, 69–71
Patient-centred, 34, 40–42
Perfectionism, 36, 61, 70
Performance-based, 41, 53
Personal identity, 28, 33, 34
Personhood, viii, 2, 4, 10–12, 19, 20, 32–43, 52–55, 59–61, 63, 67–71
Political philosophy, 3
Positive approaches, 5, 6, 10
Processual death, 23, 50

R

Rape, 8, 30
Relational, 19–21, 27, 31, 32, 37, 39, 43, 57
Relational abilities, 32
Relationalism, 31
Relational virtues, 36, 37, 53
Relationships, 6, 10, 11, 18, 21, 22, 27–32, 34, 37, 50, 52, 57–59, 65, 66
Religious, 4, 6, 11, 18–20, 52, 56
Responsibilities, 25, 28, 36, 38, 39, 43, 53, 54, 68
Rosen, M., 2, 4, 6–10, 18

S

Senses, vii, 6–8, 10, 37
Sentience, 58
Severely mentally disabled individuals, 63–71
Singer, P., 5, 62, 64, 65, 70
Slavery, 8
Solidarity, 28–32, 38, 39, 43, 52, 57–59, 65, 66
Status dignity, 7–10, 42, 43, 54

Stem cell research, 3
Stigmatize, 8
Stoics, 2, 18
Subordination, 52
Suffering, 48–51, 53–55, 60
Sympathy, 18, 28, 29, 53, 61, 70

T

Tangwa, G., 12, 54, 55
Teleological frame, 51
Thick concepts, 39, 60, 67
Torture, 8

U

Ubuntu, 11, 27
Unconditional respect, 53, 68, 69, 71
Universal Declaration of Human Rights, 1, 69
Utilitarianism, 51, 52

V

Value theory, 26, 42
Virtues, 7–9, 11, 29, 31, 34–37, 42, 53–55, 60, 61, 67, 69, 70
Vitality, viii, 2, 4, 10, 11, 19–26, 43, 48–51, 56–57, 63–64, 70
Voluntary euthanasia, 12, 47, 48, 50–55, 70, 71

W

Waldron, J., 18, 31
Welfare, 28–30, 32, 39, 52, 58, 59, 65
Well being, 27, 38, 39, 52–54, 60, 61, 67, 69
Wiredu, K., 4, 33, 34, 36, 53, 54

Printed in the United States
by Baker & Taylor Publisher Services